Crafting
with the
New Ribbons

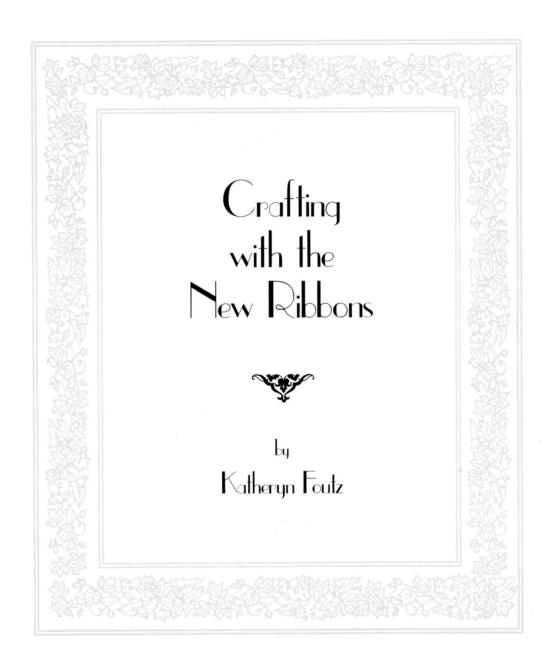

Crafting with the New Ribbons

by

Katheryn Foutz

Sterling Publishing Co., Inc. New York
A Sterling/Chapelle Book

For information on where to purchase specialty items in this book please write to: Chapelle Ltd., Customer Service Department, 204 25th Street, Ogden, Utah 84401

Library of Congress Cataloging-in Publication Data

Foutz, Katheryn.
    Crafting with the new ribbons / Katheryn Foutz.
        p.   cm.
    "A Sterling/Chapelle book."
    Includes index.
    ISBN 0-8069-1384-3
    1. Embroidery—Patterns. 2. Ribbon work. I. Title.
TT771.F65   1995
746. 44—dc20   95-16329
                                     CIP

10 9 8 7 6 5 4 3 2 1
Published by Sterling Publishing Company, Inc.
387 Park Avenue South, New York, N.Y. 10016
© 1995 by Chapelle Ltd.
Distributed in Canada by Sterling Publishing
$^{c}/_{o}$ Canadian Manda Group, One Atlantic Avenue, Suite 105
Toronto, Ontario, Canada M6K 3E7
Distributed in Great Britain and Europe by Cassell PLC
Wellington House, 125 Strand, London WC2R 0BB, England
Distributed in Australia by Capricorn Link (Australia) Pty Ltd.
P.O. Box 6651, Baulkham Hills, Business Center, NSW 2153, Australia
Printed in Hong Kong
All rights reserved

Sterling ISBN 0-8069-1384-3

For Chapelle Ltd.

Owner
Jo Packham

Staff

Malissa Boatwright   Rebecca Christensen
Amber Fuller   Holly Fuller
Cherie Hanson   Holly Hollingsworth
Susan Jorgensen   Susan Laws
Amanda McPeck   Barbara Milburn
Leslie Ridenour   Cindy Rooks
Cindy Stoekle   Kellie Valentine-Cracas
Ryanne Webster   Nancy Whitley

Photography
Kevin Dilley
for Hazen Photography

Portraits
Jeannie Marie Cunningham

About the Author

Katheryn Tidwell Foutz comes from a family in which talent in the arts is a prominent characteristic. Classical music, dance, and love of literature, as well as the creative arts flourished in her childhood environment. She began to sew at the age of nine and started her adventures into embroidery at the age of ten in the form of a sunday school sampler. From this background, along with a love of nature, she developed an eye for, and sensitivity to, beauty and her dynamic creativity. It has only taken her all her life to become an overnight success.

Over the last ten years, Katheryn's design talents have evolved from sewing and needle-crafts to woodworking, clay and fabric sculpting, painting and floral design, with a love of ribbons and Victorian ribbon work reflected through all of these mediums.

Along the way, Katheryn has done creative consultant work and written a series of books and project kits. She has done commission work for many prominent companies in the industry. She is currently working on a series of magazine articles and books on ribbon embroidery. Additionally, she teaches a variety of classes and seminars throughout California as well as across the United States.

In design, as in life, Katheryn believes in turning her stumbling blocks into stepping stones, and that you should never fret over making a mistake, but that you should find joy in having created a new variation.

Her most delightful creations are a collaborative work in progress with her husband, Kyle. Their wonderful and amazing children are Rileigh Anne, age 12; Jason, age 8; and Katelyn, age 4.

From the Author

Coming from a very musical family, my life has always been enriched by harmony. I look and listen for music in the things I create. There is harmony in designing and it is something that you feel more than you hear.

A bad note is usually obvious, and some melodies are beautiful or even haunting. As in music, I believe that a good design is emotional and should make you feel something. Sometimes I think that a design is finished and yet I hear nothing. Until a design sings sweet music, I know something is not right. Most of the designs in this book were drawn from a love of the harmony and beauty in nature. Things that I learned to appreciate with my family.

I would like to acknowledge a few people who helped me to make this book possible. Special thanks to the music of Dan Fogelberg and Kurt Bestor, that continuously inspired me; to Bonnie Stout and Bonni Raine for being those extra pairs of hands I'm always needing; to Jess and RaNae Morris for keeping my horizon balanced; to Jo Packham and the people at Chapelle Ltd. and Sterling Publishing Co. for their incredible style and patience. Finally, I wish to extend a big hug and kiss to Kyle, Rileigh, Jason, and Katelyn for the love, support, dishes, laundry, and many quick dinners. Thanks for holding on so tightly to that kite string.

Contents

About Ribbons

Silk vs. Sylk

The most common ribbons used for ribbon embroidery are silk ribbons or a silk like synthetic ribbon commonly known as SYLK. They come in a variety of widths and colors.

Silk ribbon for embroidery has been around for hundreds of years. It feels beautiful, looks beautiful, but it is delicate and has to be handled carefully. Heirloom SYLK ribbon feels beautiful, looks beautiful, and is more durable and easier to care for and less expensive than traditional silk ribbon.

Textured Ribbons

Textured ribbons are now readily available due to the new wave of ribbon embroidery. Many companies carry entire lines of textured ribbons and glitzy trims that can be used. The important thing to remember when using these ribbons is that you must use a larger needle with a fatter body to create a hole large enough for this heavier ribbon to pass through. Sometimes it is necessary to hand-tack the end of your ribbon on the back side of the stitched piece rather than tie a knot to eliminate the bulk a knot creates.

Variegated Ribbons

Variegated ribbons have an old-world look and come in a variety of colors that wash from dark to light as the color is carried across the surface of the ribbon. Many companies supply a wide assortment of variegated ribbons as well.

Bias-Cut Ribbons

These ribbons are made from large widths of fabric cut into strips on the bias (diagonal grain). The outstanding characteristic of bias-cut ribbons is their elasticity, which adds a wonderful new dimension to the stitches it is used in. These ribbons are then hand-dyed to achieve wonderful color variations. They are a bit more delicate than normal woven-edge ribbons as they have a bias *cut* raw edge.

Hand-Dyed Ribbons

Beautiful hand-dyed silk and bias-cut ribbons for embroidery are also available in an unlimited variety and combinations of colors. White ribbon is wet, dipped in one or more colors of fabric dye, then hung to dry. You can try this procedure yourself or purchase them from any number of manufacturers.

Choosing Your Color Themes

Choose colors that you love and feel comfortable with. It is a good idea to purchase ribbon colors in threes: a light, medium and dark shade.

The color themes in this book are mostly muted natural earth tones with an emphasis on beige and gold, and texture over color. There is something simple yet elegant about working within this color range.

A very elegant look can be achieved by using like colors such as ivory on ivory, or white on white. Black ribbon on a black blouse has a stunning effect. Choose colors that reflect who you are. Bring out the dramatic in that drab blouse. Recycle some romance into your old wearables.

About Needles

Chenille

A long needle with a large eye and a sharp point. Sizes 18 to 22 are the most useful for ribbon embroidery.

Crewel or Embroidery

A needle with a sharp point and a long narrow eye is used mostly for basic floss embroidery and hand stitching.

Tapestry

A blunt-ended needle with a large eye. Used in ribbon work especially to avoid snagging threads. Sizes 18 to 24 are the most practical for the projects in this book.

Darner

A great needle for stitching with cords or heavy-textured ribbons. It is a very long needle with a large eye.

Beading Needle

These needles are very fine, long needles with long narrow eyes. They are suitable for threading tiny beads onto fine floss.

STITCHING TIP: Keep several needles on hand, threaded with different colors or textures of ribbon. This creates a "palate" of ribbons at your fingertips. Rather than threading and unthreading the same needle, work from your palate.

Beginnings and Endings

Threading the Needle

To cut down the amount of wear and tear on the silk ribbons, work with 14" lengths at a time. Cut the end of the ribbon at a diagonal and thread it through a needle with a large eye, depending on the width and texture of the ribbon.

Needle Lock

"Lock" the ribbon onto the needle by poking the needle through the center of the ribbon, approximately $\frac{1}{2}$" from one end; now pull on the opposite end of the ribbon to lock the ribbon onto the eye of the needle.

Loosen Up!

Work with, not against, the ribbon. Work or wrap loose, relaxed stitches, not as tight as floss embroidery stitching. These ribbons want to fluff, curl, and roll, adding a wonderful dimension to your designs. You can control these tendencies, however, by holding the ribbon against the fabric with your thumb, as you pull the ribbon through to the back side of the fabric you are working on.

Tailor's Awl

Some wider-textured ribbons need some help to stitch through fabric. A tailor's awl is used in these instances to pierce through the fabric, creating and opening large enough to accommodate larger-textured ribbons. Pierce the fabric just before you insert the needle.

Knotting Off vs. Tying

To knot the ribbon, simply tie a small knot as close as possible to the end of the ribbon and trim off any excess. With very thick or textured ribbon, hand-stitch the end down to the back side of the fabric with a needle and thread.

When using silk or SYLK ribbons, finish your design by taking two small back-stitches, one on top of the other, then trim away the excess. Apply a small dot of liquid fray preventor on the knot or backstitch if you are going to be washing the stitched piece frequently.

Design-Transferring Methods

Eyeball It

Use this method to transfer simple designs. Basically, look at the original design and draw a guide freehand on your fabric.

Netting

Lay a piece of netting over your pattern. (Make a photocopy of the pattern to preserve the original in the book.) Trace a simple outline of the design onto the netting. Then, lay the netting onto the fabric and redraw the pattern, using a fabric marker. This will leave small dots on the fabric.

Cut It Out!

Trace the outline of the design on a piece of paper. Cutout the paper design along the outlined edge. Lay the cut out on your fabric and draw around the cut edge with a fabric marker.

Sunlight

For a natural light-box effect, trace the design on a piece of paper with black ink. Tape the paper onto a sun-lit window. Hold or tape the fabric in place over the design and trace the design onto the fabric with an erasable fabric marker.

Fabric Marking Pens

It is recommended that you use an air-soluble fabric marker when using any of these techniques. The markings of air-soluble fabric markers are usually visible from 24 to 72 hours. If you choose not to use these types of markers, only transfer general stitch placement and shapes to avoid any permanent pattern markings on your fabric. Use the following example as a guide.

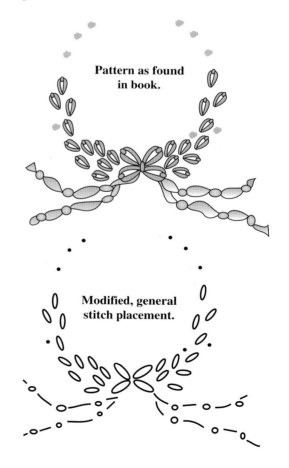

Pattern as found in book.

Modified, general stitch placement.

Ribbon-Embroidery Stitches & Techniques

Bead Couching

This is a small stitch used to tack long loose lengths of ribbon. Using a beading needle and floss, bring the needle up from the back of the fabric and through the ribbon or cording to be tacked. Thread a small seed bead onto the floss and return back down through the fabric.

Bullion-Tipped Lazy Daisy Stitch

This is the basic LAZY DAISY STITCH, with a simple variation. After you have made your loop and are ready to make a small anchoring stitch to hold the loop secure, wrap the needle gently but flatly three times with the ribbon close to the sharp point of the needle. This stitch makes a realistic-looking leaf.

Cascading

With a needle threaded with ribbon, stitch loose, twisted RIBBON STITCHES placed as desired.

Chain Stitch

Begins the same as the LAZY DAISY STITCH, except it is continuous. Instead of taking an anchor stitch at the end of the loop, continue on as though you were making another Lazy Daisy.

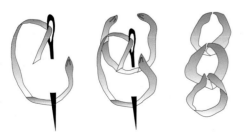

Cretan Stitch

Bring the needle up at A on the inner stitching line. Insert it at B on the outer stitching line; bring it out slightly below and to the left at C, keeping the thread to the right. Then, insert the needle at D and bring it up at E, keeping the thread to the right.

Feather Stitch

See FLY STITCH.

Fly Stitch

Embroider a "Y"-shape by inserting the needle in the second stitch down and to the left. Alternating this stitch left and right produces the FEATHER STITCH.

French Knot

Bring the needle up and wrap the ribbon loosely two or three times around the needle close to the sharp point. Hold the ribbon off to one side gently as you insert the needle next to the entry hole. Hold this knot with your finger until the ribbon is pulled all the way through to the back of the fabric.

Lazy Daisy Stitch

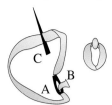

Bring the needle up at A, down through fabric at B, forming a loose loop. To hold the loop in place, go up at C and down on other side of ribbon, forming a STRAIGHT STITCH over loop.

Puffed Ribbon Stitch

Almost identical to the RIBBON STITCH, only you pierce the ribbon and slide it up towards the entry point to puff it, then, go back down through the fabric.

Ribbon Stitch

Bring the needle up through the fabric. Lay the ribbon flat against the fabric. Pierce the center of the ribbon on your way back down through the fabric to create a soft curl at the end of this stitch. Pull the ribbon through gently so that you do not loose this soft curl.

Ribbon Weave Stitch

Bring the ribbon up through the fabric and make lengthwise rows of STRAIGHT STITCHES stitched side by side. Begin along the top left edge of these lengthwise rows and bring the ribbon up from the back of the fabric and weave the ribbon over and under each lengthwise stitch of ribbon. When you get to the end of the row, drop down one ribbon width and weave your way back across the ribbon, alternating over and under the lengthwise strips. Continue in this manner until the entire area is woven.

Rolled Straight Stitch

Bring the ribbon up through the fabric. Roll the needle between your thumb and forefinger until the ribbon creates a smooth spiral; then, travel across the fabric the desired distance and bring the needle back down through the fabric. It is not necessary to unroll the needle between stitches.

Satin Stitch

These are simply STRAIGHT STITCHES worked side by side.

Spider Web Rose

Using embroidery floss or narrow ribbon, stitch a "Y"-shape. Add a straight stitch on either side of the "Y", forming five spokes. Each stitch should be approximately the same length. With a needle threaded with 4mm or 7mm ribbon, bring the needle up next to the center of the "Y". Twist the ribbon a few times by rolling the needle between your fingers; then, begin winding the ribbon alternately over and under the spokes of the "Y" stitches. Begin with a dark shade, gradually working toward a lighter shade as you reach the outer edges of the rose. Be sure to keep your stitches loose and full. Continue in this manner until the anchor stitches are completely covered and hidden from view.

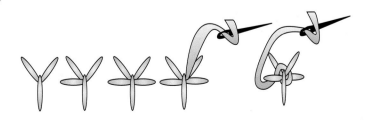

Stacked Fly Stitch

This is a group of FLY STITCHES stitched vertically to form a leaf shape.

Stem Stitch

This stitch is worked from left to right. Keeping the ribbon to the left of the needle, come up in the center and to the right of the previous stitch, making slightly slanting stitches.

Straight Stitch

Bring the needle up through the fabric. Travel along the desired distance; then, bring the needle back down through the fabric.

Twisted Bullion-Tipped Lazy Daisy Stitch

Worked basically the same as the BULLION- TIPPED LAZY DAISY STITCH, except you cross the ribbon over the needle, twisting the loop in the first stage of the stitch; then, proceed anchoring the twisted loop as in the Bullion-Tipped version.

Two-Stitch Twisted Rose

Using a 14" length of ribbon, bring the needle up through the fabric. Raise the needle straight up above the fabric. Roll the needle between your thumb and index finger, turning the ribbon in a clockwise

direction until the ribbon forms a spiraled tube with small spaces between the spirals. Allow the needle to lower as the spirals take up the length of the ribbon. Pinch the center point of the spiraled ribbon and pull it over to one side. Begin to insert the needle back down into the fabric approximately $1/4$" from the entry point. Stop pushing just before the needle is completely through the fabric. Release the coil. The ribbon will now twist around itself and form a double coil. Run your fingers lightly down the length of the coil. Finish pulling the needle through the fabric to form the rose. Stop pulling when the rose becomes the desired size. With a needle threaded with beading floss or matching thread, take a small tack stitch up through the center of the rose. A 14" length of ribbon will make approximately two to three roses.

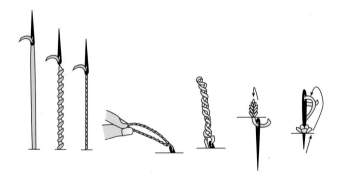

Wave Stitch

This is worked around a base stitch of floss, such as a STRAIGHT STITCH. The ribbon is brought up from the back of the fabric and looped around the floss without piercing the floss or the fabric, except at the beginning and end of the stitch.

Basic Bud

Make a point by crossing one end of a 3" length of ribbon down and across the other end of the ribbon. For a rolled bud, roll the ribbon from the right edge toward the left edge. Stitch to secure the roll.

Folded Leaf

Make a point by crossing one end of a 3½" length of ribbon down and across the other end of the ribbon. Run a gathering stitch across the bottom of the ribbon just below the intersection of the crossing ends. Where you place the gathering stitches determines the length of the leaf. Pull the gathering thread tightly and knot to secure.

Folded & Rolled Rose

Cut a 9" length of 7mm to 9mm ribbon. Fold one end of the ribbon down at a right angle, creating a post to hold onto. Fold the folded end in half. Stitch this in place securely with thread. Continue rolling and folding ribbon as shown, stitching to secure as you go. When you have folded and rolled at least half of the 9" length of ribbon, hand-stitch a gathering stitch along the bottom edge of the remaining length of ribbon. Pull the gathers tightly and wrap this gathered section around the folded rose. Stitch in place to secure.

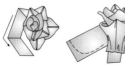

Multiple-Petaled Flower

Make a BASIC BUD. Make SINGLE PETALS. Wrap and overlap petals around bud; securing with stitches at the base. Make MULTI-PETALED SECTIONS. Wrap and overlap lengths of MULTI-PETAL SECTIONS around the bud/single petals and secure with small stitches at the base of the flower.

Multiple-Petaled Section

Using a disappearing-ink fabric marker, mark a 12½" length of ribbon at 4" intervals, beginning and ending ¼" from raw ends. Run a hand-gathering stitch in a semicircular shape within each interval. Pull the gathering thread tightly so that each petal measures about 1¼". Knot thread to secure.

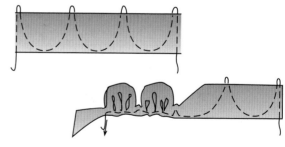

Single Petal

Run a hand-gathering stitch along one long edge and the sides of a 4" length of ribbon. Pull the gathering thread tightly until the ribbon measures 1¼". Knot the thread to secure. Repeat to make as many petals as required. Note: For a smooth, rounded petal, the length of the ribbon should equal the width of the ribbon multiplied by three. For a cupped petal, the length should equal the width multiplied by two. For a very ruffled petal, the length should equal the width multiplied by four.

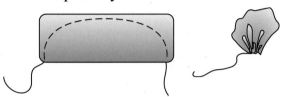

Stuffed-Fabric Berries

Cut a small circle of fabric. Run a hand-gathering stitch along the raw edge. Pull the gathering thread slightly and fill the center with a small amount of stuffing. Pull the gathering thread tightly and stitch to secure.

Stuffed-Ribbon Berries

Cut a 4" length of 1" ribbon or amount specified in instructions. With right sides facing, fold it in half and stitch the short ends together $1/4$" from raw edges, forming a tube. Turn the ribbon right side out and run a hand-gathering stitch along the top long edge. Pull the gathering thread tightly and stitch to secure. Run a gathering stitch along the bottom edge of the ribbon. Fill the berry firmly with stuffing. Pull the bottom gathering thread tightly and stitch to secure.

Wrapped Bud

Cut a 4" length of ribbon. Lay a previously made bud in the center of the ribbon length. Cross one end of the 4" length of ribbon down and across the other end of the ribbon, wrapping the bud in the center. Run a gathering stitch across this wrapped piece. Pull the gathering thread tightly and wrap the thread around the base. Knot to secure.

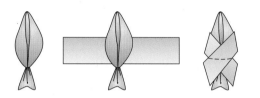

Beaded Accents

Beaded accents give things an unexpected touch of elegance and can be extremely simple to create. Using a beading needle and floss, simply stitch beads individually or in clusters of two to three beads per stitch.

Fabric-Edge Fraying

The best results are achieved when using a loosely woven fabric. Cut the fabric along the straight grain and pull the fibers along this edge to fray. Continue pulling threads one at a time until the desired length of fringe is achieved. Trim edges if necessary.

Mitering Corners

Hem outside edges of item to be mitered 1/4". Fold each corner down as shown. Then, fold each side in and stitch to secure.

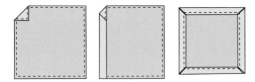

Painted Accents

To achieve a wonderful gilded highlight to desired projects, rub the raised edges of your embroidered piece with acrylic gold paint with a cotton swab or your finger.

Ribbon Pin Weaving

This is a process of creating your own fabric by weaving together a collection of ribbons, laces, and trims. Transfer the pattern onto a sheet of paper and lay it right side up on your work surface (a sheet of foam core or cardboard is recommended). Lay fusible webbing over pattern . Pin ribbons and trims side by side in a lengthwise direction in neat straight lines; pin or tape in place along the top edge. Also pin or tape the bottom edge about 1" below the pattern outline. Continue to lay strips of ribbon until the entire pattern has been covered. Repeat this process in a crosswise direction, pinning the left side edge only and leaving the right side free for weaving. Weave ribbons one at a time over and under each lengthwise strip. It is helpful to thread a large blunt needle with each ribbon length as you weave it. Another favorite trick is to take a bamboo skewer and weave it over and under the ribbons, creating a space for you to easily thread the ribbon through. After you have finished weaving your ribbons, fuse the ribbons together with iron-on fusible webbing, following manufacturer's instructions. Remove pins and tape as the edges are pressed. Remove the woven ribbons from the work surface and cut pattern along edge and stitch as desired.

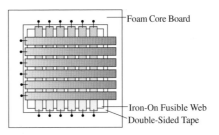

Foam Core Board

Iron-On Fusible Web
Double-Sided Tape

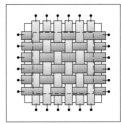

Stenciling

Secure a purchased stencil onto item to be stenciled with tape. Apply paint to the stencil brush and blot it dry, drier than you think it should be so that the paint will not bleed under the edges of the stencil. Paint the item through the cut out portions of the stencil.

Ribbons on Ribbon

Ribbons on Ribbon

Stitches & Techniques
BULLION-TIPPED LAZY DAISY STITCH
FABRIC-EDGE FRAYING

Materials
21" of 1⁷/₈" tan velvet ribbon
8" x 12" piece of tan, loosely woven fabric
4mm tan silk ribbon
Disappearing-ink fabric marker
Large-eyed needle (darner)
Scissors
Five 9" beeswax candles
Small bunch of dried flowers or herbs

Directions
1. Using the transfer method of your choice (page 13), lightly transfer the design onto the velvet ribbon with the fabric marker.

2. Using the BULLION-TIPPED LAZY DAISY STITCH (page 14), begin in the center of the ribbon and stitch the pattern down to the end of the ribbon. Repeat on the opposite side.

3. Cut each end of the velvet ribbon into a point.

4. Fray the edges of the 8" x 12" fabric rectangle following the FABRIC-EDGE FRAYING technique (page 18). Trim the edges so that finished size is 6" x 10", including a ¹/₂" frayed edge.

5. Wrap the fabric around the candles and tie with the embroidered velvet ribbon. Slide the small bunch of flowers or herbs just under the knot.

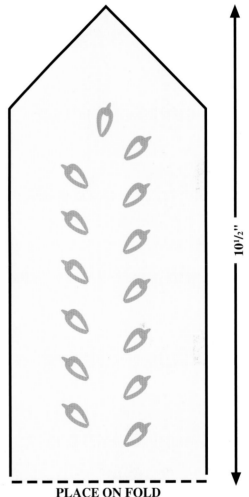

10¹/₂"

PLACE ON FOLD
(Flop pattern on opposite side.)

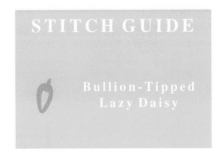

STITCH GUIDE

Bullion-Tipped
Lazy Daisy

Bows 'n' Berries

Bows 'n' Berries

Stitches & Techniques

BEADED ACCENTS
CASCADING
FRENCH KNOT
LAZY DAISY STITCH
STACKED FLY STITCH
STEM STITCH

Materials

One 8" x 10" bleached burlap bag
5mm burgundy sheer ribbon
3mm blue-green textured ribbon
1.5mm brown rayon ribbon
1.5mm green rayon ribbon
1 yard of ½" gold-edged, ivory sheer ribbon
Burgundy/blue seed beads
Disappearing-ink fabric marker
Large-eyed needle (darner)
Beading needle and thread
Scissors

Directions

1. Using the transfer method of your choice (page 13), transfer the design onto the bag front.

2. Use the STEM STITCH (page 16) with 1.5mm brown ribbon to form the stem, the STACKED FLY STITCH (page 16) with 3mm ribbon to form the leaves, and the BULLION-TIPPED LAZY DAISY (page 14) with 1.5mm green ribbon to form the berry tops. Fill in the berries with FRENCH KNOTS (page 14) using 5mm burgundy sheer ribbon; intersperse with a few beads, hand stitched in place with a beading needle and thread.

3. For the bow, stitch two large, loose LAZY DAISY STITCHES (page 15), forming the bow loops. After each LAZY DAISY STITCH, trim ribbon ends on back side of fabric and tack down. Re-thread ribbon and take a small stitch at the center of the bow loops. Adjust ribbon so that it is centered and tie a half knot at the center of the bow loops. One at a time, thread needle with bow ends and CASCADE (page 14) ends as shown in photo.

Bows 'n' Berries Pattern

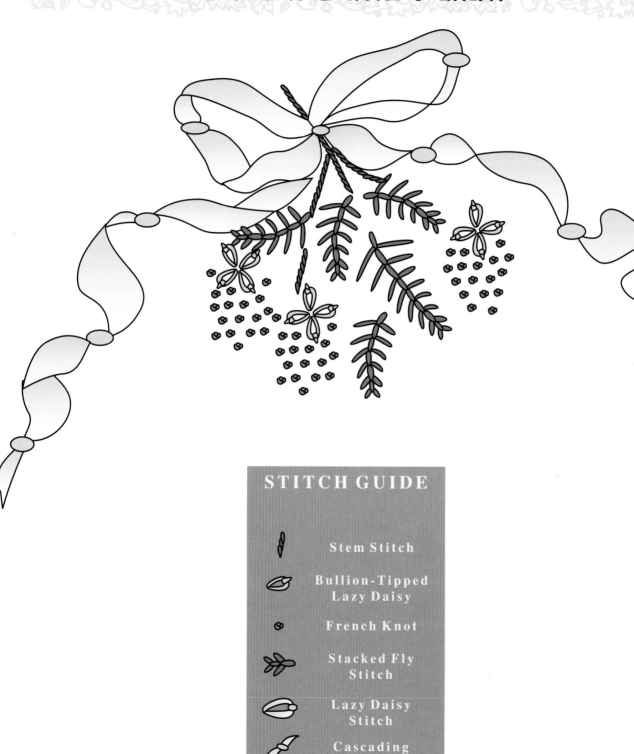

STITCH GUIDE

Stem Stitch

Bullion-Tipped
Lazy Daisy

French Knot

Stacked Fly
Stitch

Lazy Daisy
Stitch

Cascading

24

STITCH GUIDE

Straight Stitch

Cretan Stitch

Cascading

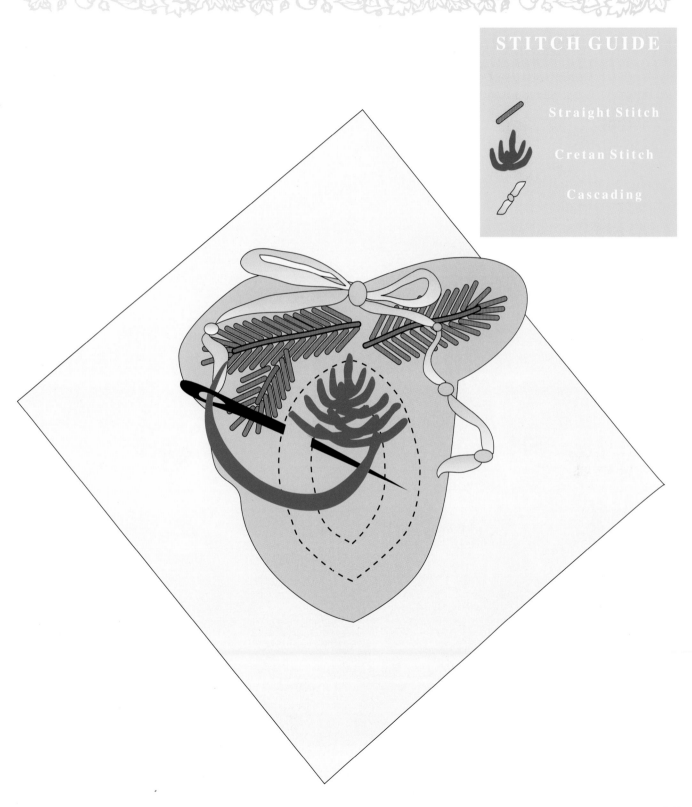

Mountain Treasures

Mountain Treasures

Stitches & Techniques
CASCADING
CRETAN STITCH
STRAIGHT STITCH

Materials
One 9" x 10" burlap drawstring bag
One 8" square of brown woven fabric
$5^1/_2$" square of antique lace or doily
$1^1/_2$ yards of $^3/_8$" brown/gold ribbon
$^3/_4$ yard of $^1/_8$" gold ribbon
1.5mm green/brown rayon ribbon
Thin green rayon cording
One 6" embroidery hoop
Tailor's awl
Disappearing-ink fabric marker
Large-eyed needle (darner)
Needle and sewing thread
Scissors

Directions
1. Place the square of brown fabric in the embroidery hoop. Using the transfer method of your choice (page 13), transfer the design onto the fabric.

2. Following the instructions for the CRETAN STITCH (page 14) embroider the pinecone with $^3/_8$" ribbon; use the tailor's awl to pierce the fabric before you make each stitch, to create an opening large enough for the ribbon to pass fairly easily through the fabric.

3. Make the branch by taking three large STRAIGHT STITCHES (page 16) with the 1.5mm green/brown ribbon. Add pine needles by repeatedly taking STRAIGHT STITCHES with green cording, as shown in photo and pattern.

4. Using the gold ribbon, tie a $2^1/_2$" bow and hand-stitch it in place at the top of the branch. One at a time, thread needle with bow ends and CASCADE (page 14) ends as shown in photo.

5. Cut $^1/_2$" around the design and pull loose threads, creating a frayed effect.

6. Center and hand-stitch a $5^1/_2$" square of antique lace to the bag front. Center and machine- or hand-stitch embroidered fabric to the bag front, stitching around the design to secure.

Sunflower Tote

Sunflower Tote

Stitches & Techniques
RIBBON WEAVE STITCH
STEM STITCH
STRAIGHT STITCH

Materials
One 15" x 11" burlap bag
1½ yards of ⅜" medium-brown velvet ribbon
1½ yards of ⅜" dark-brown velvet ribbon
7mm bronze rayon ribbon
7mm gray-green cotton ribbon
7mm khaki-green cotton ribbon
3mm multicolored-green textured ribbon
Disappearing-ink fabric marker
Large-eyed needle (darner)
Larger-eyed, fat-bodied needle to accommodate
   the velvet ribbon
Tailor's awl
Scissors

Directions
1. Using the transfer method of your choice (page 13), transfer the design onto bag front with the fabric marker. Using velvet ribbon threaded onto a large-eyed, fat-bodied needle, begin to stitch and weave the sunflower centers, following the guidelines for the RIBBON WEAVE STITCH (page 15). Note: The flower on the left is woven with two shades of ribbon and the flower on the right is woven in one shade only.

2. Use the photo and pattern as a color guide. Stitch petals using 7mm bronze ribbon with the STRAIGHT STITCH (page 16); stitch leaves using 7mm gray-green ribbon and khaki-green ribbon with the STRAIGHT STITCH. Stitch the stems and leaf centers with 3mm green ribbon, using the STEM STITCH (page 16).

STITCH GUIDE

Stem Stitch

Straight Stitch

Ribbon Weave
Stitch

Sunflower Tote Pattern

STITCH GUIDE

Puffed Berries

Straight Stitch

Simple Elegance Vest Pattern

Simple Elegance Vest

Simple Elegance Vest

Stitches & Techniques
STUFFED-FABRIC BERRIES
STRAIGHT STITCH

Materials
One large vest with a loosely woven linen front
  and pockets
Six 1¼"-diameter fabric circles
Scraps of antique lace (to fill pocket)
4mm taupe silk ribbon
3mm ivory textured ribbon
3mm gray-green textured ribbon
Thin gold cording
Disappearing-ink fabric marker
Large-eyed needle (darner)
Beading needle and floss
Scissors
Gold acrylic paint
Small paintbrush or cotton swab

Directions
1. Using the transfer method of your choice (page 13), transfer the design onto the vest front with the fabric marker.

2. Thread needle with gold cording and tack into place with beading floss, forming leaf outlines and vines. Fill in leaves with STRAIGHT STITCHES (page 16) using 3mm gray-green and 4mm taupe ribbon; see photo and pattern for color and stitch placement.

3. Make six STUFFED-FABRIC BERRIES (page 18) from the fabric circles. Paint the berries with gold paint; let dry.

4. Hand-stitch the berries in place on vest with beading floss.

5. Stitch one long STRAIGHT STITCH using gold cording along opposite pocket welt; tack with beading floss to secure. Fill pocket with antique lace and tack to secure.

Oak Leaf & Acorn Table Runner

Oak Leaf & Acorn Table Runner

Stitches & Techniques
CHAIN STITCH
FRENCH KNOT
RIBBON STITCH
STRAIGHT STITCH

Materials
15½" x 56" piece of loosely woven fabric
15½" x 56" piece of taupe moire taffeta
Two 6" tassels
7mm gray textured mesh ribbon
7mm taupe textured ribbon
3mm light-gray textured ribbon
Thin ivory cording
10"-diameter embroidery hoop
Disappearing-ink fabric marker
Large-eyed needle (darner)
Needle and sewing thread
Beading needle and floss
Scissors

Directions
All seams are ½".

1. At one end of the woven piece, 5½" from short edge and 7¾" from long edge, mark the placement for the center of the design. Using the transfer method of your choice (page 13), transfer the design onto the fabric with the fabric marker. Place the fabric in the embroidery hoop.

2. Stitch acorns with 7mm taupe ribbon using the RIBBON STITCH (page 15). Stitch one long STRAIGHT STITCH (page 16) for each of the stems using thin ivory cording; then fill in the caps with FRENCH KNOTS (page 14) using thin ivory cording.

3. Stitch the oak leaves with 7mm gray ribbon using the RIBBON STITCH.

4. Stitch one long STRAIGHT STITCH using 3mm gray ribbon; tack with beading floss to secure.

5. Stitch three small CHAIN STITCHES (page 14) to form the stem of each leaf.

6. Using a 24" length of 7mm taupe ribbon, tie a 2¾" bow. Hand-stitch bow at top center of acorns and oak leaves. Arrange tails and tack with beading floss to secure. Note: Repeat Steps 1-6 to stitch design on opposite end of table runner if desired.

7. Cut ends of woven fabric at diagonals to form a point at each end; see diagram below. Using woven fabric as a pattern, cut diagonal ends of moire taffeta piece.

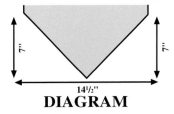

DIAGRAM

8. With right sides of fabric pieces facing, machine-stitch together, leaving a 5" opening in one side seam. Turn right side out through opening. Hand-stitch opening closed. Press.

9. Hand-stitch one tassel to each point.

STITCH GUIDE

Chain Stitch

French Knot

Straight Stitch

Ribbon Stitch

Basic Christmas Stocking

Materials

¹/₂ yard of ivory fabric
¹/₂ yard of ivory muslin
12" of 1" ivory ribbon
Ivory sewing thread
Sewing machine

Directions

All seams are ¹/₂".

1. From fabric, cut one stocking front, one stocking back, and two 4¹/₄" x 9" pieces for stocking cuff. From muslin, cut one stocking front and one stocking back for lining.

2. With right sides of fabric pieces facing and edges aligned, machine-stitch together, leaving the top edge open. Trim seams; turn.

3. With right sides of the lining pieces facing and edges aligned, machine-stitch together, leaving the top edge open and an opening in the side seam above the heel. Do not turn.

4. Slide the lining over the stocking, right sides together. Stitch around the top edge of the stocking. Turn the stocking right side out through the side opening in the lining. Slip-stitch the opening closed. Slide the lining inside the stocking.

5. Fold the 12" length of 1" ivory ribbon in half and tie the ends together in a knot. Hand-stitch the knot to the back side seam above the heel, just inside the top edge of the stocking, forming a hanger.

6. Embellish one 4¹/₄" x 9" cuff piece as desired; see projects on pages 37, 43, and 46. With right sides of cuff pieces facing and edges aligned, stitch together, leaving a 3" opening in one side seam. Clip corners. Turn the cuff right side out through the side opening. Slip-stitch the opening closed.

7. Hand-stitch the cuff to the top edge of the stocking front.

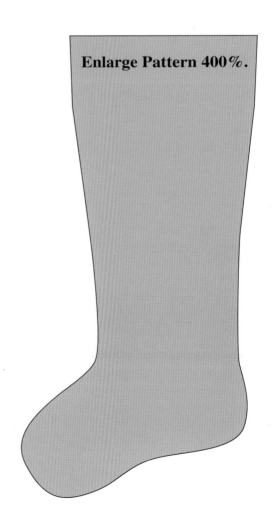

Enlarge Pattern 400%.

Holly & Ivory Cuff

Holly & Ivory Cuff

Stitches & Techniques
STUFFED-FABRIC BERRIES
RIBBON STITCH
RIBBON WEAVING
STRAIGHT STITCH

Materials
Completed stocking (page 37)
1 yard of 1" beige, canvas, gold edged, wired
   ribbon
4 yards of $1/2$" gold acetate ribbon
7mm green rayon ribbon
Three 1"-diameter ivory silk fabric circles
$4^{1}/_{4}$" x 9" piece of fusible webbing
Small amount of stuffing
Tailor's awl
Disappearing-ink fabric marker
Large-eyed needle (darner)
Scissors

Directions
1. Weave ribbon for cuff, according to
RIBBON PIN WEAVING instructions
(page 19). Fuse woven ribbons to fabric
with fusible webbing, following manufacturer's instructions.

2. Using the transfer method of your choice
(page 13), transfer the holly design onto the
cuff with the fabric marker.

3. Stitch the holly leaves with 7mm green
ribbon using STRAIGHT STITCHES (page
16) and RIBBON STITCHES (page 15).
Use the tailor's awl to pierce holes through
the fabric when necessary.

4. Make three STUFFED-FABRIC BERRIES
(page 18) from the fabric circles and hand-
stitch them in a cluster in the center of the
holly leaves.

5. Cut a 24" length of 1" beige wired ribbon.
Tie ribbon into a 4" bow and hand-stitch it
just under the berry cluster. Arrange and
hand-tack the tails of the bow to the
stocking front.

6. Finish stocking according to basic stocking
instructions on page 37.

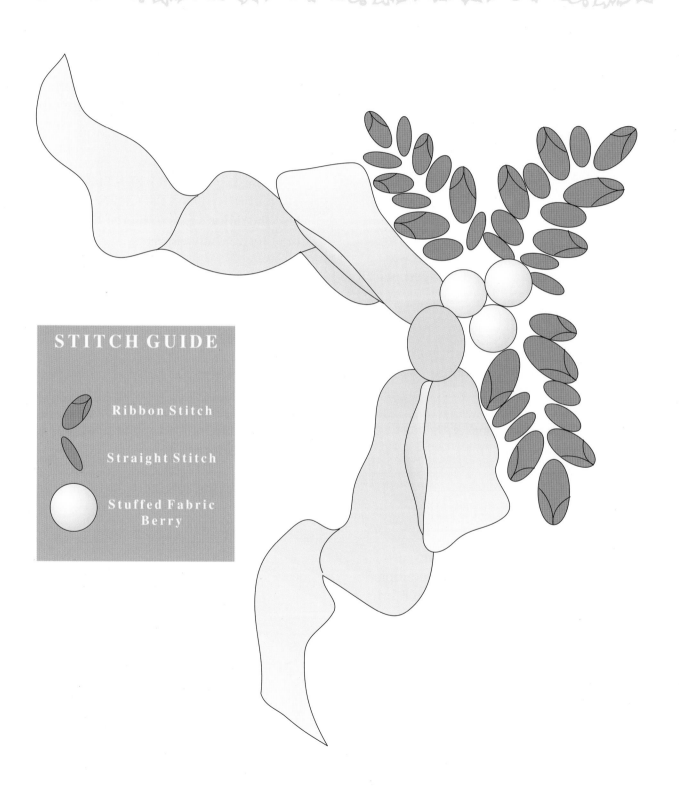

STITCH GUIDE

Ribbon Stitch

Straight Stitch

Stuffed Fabric
Berry

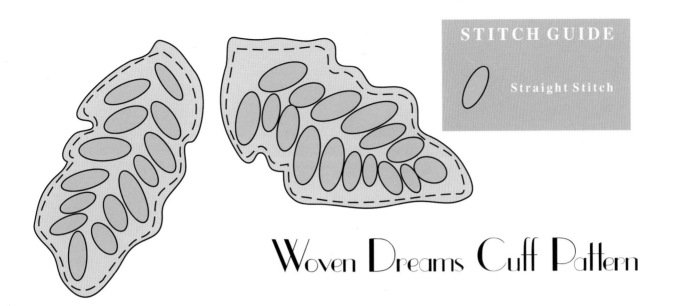

STITCH GUIDE

Straight Stitch

Woven Dreams Cuff Pattern

STITCH GUIDE

French Knot

Ribbon Stitch

Straight Stitch

Woven Wonderland Cuff Pattern

41

Woven Dreams Cuff

Woven Dreams Cuff

Stitches & Techniques
CASCADING
RIBBON WEAVING
STRAIGHT STITCH

Materials
Completed stocking (page 37)
12" of 1" beige, textured, gold-edged, wired
   ribbon
2 yards of $1/4$" ivory cording
24" of $1/2$" ivory sheer, gold-edged ribbon
$4^{1}/_{2}$ yards of $1^{1}/_{2}$" ivory sheer, gold-edged ribbon
1 yard of $1/2$" burnished, gold sheer ribbon
2 yards of 1" white sheer, gold-edged ribbon
$2^{1}/_{2}$ yards of $1/4$" metallic-gold wired ribbon
Two 10" squares of canvas fabric
Tailor's awl
One 8" embroidery hoop
Disappearing-ink fabric marker
Large-eyed needle (darner)
Scissors

Directions
1. Weave stocking front with ribbons
   according to RIBBON PIN WEAVING
   instructions (page 19).

2. Place one 10" square of canvas in
   embroidery hoop. Transfer the design onto
   the fabric using the transfer method of your
   choice (page 13) with the fabric marker.

3. Stitch the leaves with $1/4$" metallic-gold
   wired ribbon using STRAIGHT STITCHES
   (page 16). Use the tailor's awl to pierce
   holes through the fabric when necessary.

4. Remove fabric from hoop. With the right
   side up, lay the stitched fabric square over
   the remaining 10" fabric square. Machine-
   stitch the fabric squares together as close as
   possible around the outline of the stitched
   design. Cut out the design just outside the
   stitching line.

5. Tie $1/2$" ivory sheer, gold-edged ribbon into
   a 4" bow. Stitch the leaves to the bow and
   hand-stitch the bow and leaves centered 1"
   from the top edge of the stocking. Arrange
   and CASCADE (page 14) the tails of the
   bow to the stocking front.

6. Tie and drape the cording across the top
   edge of the stocking; see photo. Hand-stitch
   in place to stocking front.

Woven Wonderland Cuff

Woven Wonderland Cuff

Stitches & Techniques

FRENCH KNOT
PAINTED ACCENTS
RIBBON STITCH
RIBBON PIN WEAVING
STRAIGHT STITCH

Materials

Completed stocking (page 37)
1 yard of $1/4$" ivory cording
Assorted white, ivory, and gold ribbons in
    various sizes and textures
7mm ivory textured ribbon
$1/8$" gold braid
$1/2$" gold acetate ribbon
Metallic-gold paint
Cotton swab
Disappearing-ink fabric marker
Large-eyed needle (darner)
Beading needle and thread
Scissors

Directions

1. Weave stocking front with ribbons according to RIBBON PIN WEAVING instructions (page 19).

2. Using the transfer method of your choice (page 13), lightly transfer the design onto the cuff with the fabric marker.

3. Stitch the stems using long STRAIGHT STITCHES (page 16) with $1/8$" gold braid; tack with beading floss to secure.

4. To make leaves, alternate STRAIGHT STITCHES and RIBBON STITCHES (page 15) using 7mm ivory textured ribbon. Stitch FRENCH KNOTS (page 14) using $1/2$" gold acetate ribbon.

5. Lightly apply gold paint to the leaves with a cotton swab, accenting raised areas of the leaf. Let dry.

6. Finish stocking according to basic stocking instructions (page 37).

Hydrangea Pillow

Hydrangea Pillow

Stitches & Techniques
LAZY DAISY STITCH
PUFFED RIBBON STITCH
ROLLED STRAIGHT STITCH
STACKED FLY STITCH
STRAIGHT STITCH

Materials
5/8 yard of loosely woven fabric
12" pillow form
12" square of netting
7mm lavender and purple hand-dyed, bias-cut silk ribbon
1/4" sheer green ribbon
5mm green rayon ribbon
Taupe sewing thread
14"-diameter embroidery hoop
Disappearing-ink fabric marker
Large-eyed needle (darner)
Needle and sewing thread
Scissors

Directions
1. From fabric, cut one 19$\frac{1}{2}$" square for pillow front and two 19$\frac{1}{2}$" x 13$\frac{1}{4}$" pieces for pillow backs. Using the NETTING transfer method (page 13), transfer the design onto the pillow front. Place the pillow front in the embroidery hoop.

2. Fill the flower petal area with loose PUFFED RIBBON STITCHES (page 15) using lavender silk ribbon. Note: Each large cluster of flowers is made up of small, individual, four-petaled flowers.

3. Stitch ROLLED STRAIGHT STITCHES (page 15) using 1/4" green ribbon to form small stems within the flower.

4. Fill the stem area with closely placed STRAIGHT STITCHES (page 16) using 1/4" green ribbon.

5. To make leaves, stitch one large LAZY DAISY STITCH (page 15) at the tip of the leaf using 5mm green ribbon. Continue down the length of the leaf stitching STACKED FLY STITCHES (page 16).

6. Fold one long edge of one pillow back piece under 1/4"; double-fold edge under 1" and press. Hem folded edge. Repeat on remaining pillow back piece.

7. With right sides facing, pin pillow front to backs with raw edges aligned and hemmed edges overlapping in the center.

8. Stitch 5/8" seams completely around pillow edges. Clip corners. Turn right side out. Press.

9. Topstitch around pillow 2$\frac{1}{2}$" inside finished edge. Insert pillow form through back opening.

Hydrangea Pillow Pattern

STITCH GUIDE

Straight Stitch

Rolled Straight
Stitch

Puffed Ribbon
Stitch

Stacked Fly
Stitch

Lazy Daisy
Stitch

Ivy Clings Basket Cover

Stitches & Techniques
BULLION-TIPPED LAZY DAISY STITCH
FABRIC-EDGE FRAYING
STRAIGHT STITCH

Materials
24" square of woven fabric
$^1/_4$" green sheer ribbon
Thin green cording
Disappearing-ink fabric marker
Large-eyed needle (darner)
Beading needle and thread
Straight pins
Scissors

Directions
1. Fray the edges of the fabric square $^1/_2$" on all sides following the FABRIC-EDGE FRAYING technique (page 18). Using the transfer method of your choice (page 13), lightly transfer the design onto the fabric with the fabric marker.

2. Pin the cording in place for tendril and vine; tack with beading floss to secure.

3. Stitch the large ivy leaf with STRAIGHT STITCHES (page 16) using $^1/_4$" green ribbon. Stitch the small ivy leaves with three BULLION-TIPPED LAZY DAISY STITCHES (page 14) and two STRAIGHT STITCHES using $^1/_4$" green ribbon.

STITCH GUIDE

Bullion-Tipped Lazy Daisy

Straight Stitch

Ivy clings. . . and so does the joy that loving you brings. May the joy of old friendships cling even through the vines of old rememberings.

—*Darrin Barney*

Ivy Clings Basket Cover, Place Mat & Napkin

Ivy Clings Place Mat

Stitches & Techniques
STRAIGHT STITCH

Materials
25" x 18" piece of ivory fabric; matching thread
$1/4$" green sheer ribbon
Thin green cording
Disappearing-ink fabric marker
Large-eyed needle (darner)
Beading needle and floss
Scissors
Sewing machine

Directions

1. Fold edges of the fabric square $1/4$"; double-fold $1 1/2$". MITER corners (page 19). Press. Machine-stitch around outside folded edges.

2. Using the transfer method of your choice (page 13), lightly transfer the design onto the fabric with the fabric marker.

3. Pin the cording in place for tendrils and vine; tack with beading floss to secure.

4. Stitch the ivy leaves with STRAIGHT STITCHES (page 16) using $1/4$" green ribbon.

STITCH GUIDE

Straight Stitch

Stitches & Techniques

BULLION-TIPPED LAZY DAISY STITCH
STRAIGHT STITCH

Materials

22" square of ivory fabric; matching thread
$1/4$" green sheer ribbon
Thin green cording
Beading floss
Disappearing-ink fabric marker
Large-eyed needle (darner)
Beading needle
Scissors
Sewing machine

Directions

1. Fold edges of the fabric square $1/4$"; double-fold $3/8$" and press. Machine-stitch around outside folded edges, MITERING corners (page 19).

2. Using the transfer method of your choice (page 13), lightly transfer the design onto the fabric with the fabric marker.

3. Pin the cording in place for tendrils and vine; tack with beading floss to secure.

4. Stitch the large ivy leaf with STRAIGHT STITCHES (page 16) using $1/4$" green ribbon. Stitch the small ivy leaves with three BULLION-TIPPED LAZY DAISY STITCHES (page 14) and two STRAIGHT STITCHES using $1/4$" green ribbon.

STITCH GUIDE

Bullion-Tipped
Lazy Daisy

Straight Stitch

Acorn Box Pattern

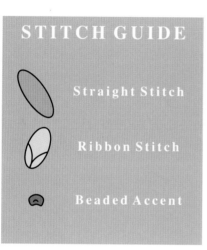

STITCH GUIDE

Straight Stitch

Ribbon Stitch

Beaded Accent

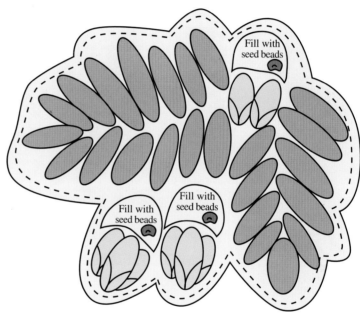

Fill with seed beads

Fill with seed beads

Fill with seed beads

Acorn Box

Acorn Box

Stitches & Techniques
BEADED ACCENTS
RIBBON STITCH
STENCILING
STRAIGHT STITCH

Materials
7"-square paper maché box with lid
Two 7" squares of fabric; matching thread
5½" square of fusible webbing
7mm taupe rayon ribbon
7mm ivory rayon ribbon
25" of ⅛" flat gold braid
24" of ⅝" flat ivory trim
Approximately 150 bronze seed beads
6" embroidery hoop
Disappearing-ink fabric marker
Large-eyed needle (darner)
Beading needle and floss
Scissors
Sewing machine
Tacky glue
Metallic-gold paint
Stencil brush
Checkerboard stencil
Masking tape
Paper towels

Directions
1. Apply gold paint to box using the STENCILING technique (page 19). Allow to dry.

2. Fuse 5½" fabric square on top of box with fusible webbing, following manufacturer's instructions.

3. Edge top of box with braid and trim; secure with glue; set box lid aside.

4. Using the transfer method of your choice (page 13), lightly transfer the design onto one of the 7" fabric squares with the fabric marker. Place the fabric in the embroidery hoop.

5. Using 7mm ivory rayon ribbon, stitch the acorns with three RIBBON STITCHES (page 15), ending near a common point.

6. Fill in acorn cap area with seed beads hand stitched in place with beading needle and floss. Stitch leaves with STRAIGHT STITCHES (page 16) using 7mm taupe rayon ribbon.

7. Remove the fabric from the hoop. With the right side up, lay the stitched fabric square over the remaining 7" fabric square. Machine-stitch the fabric squares together approximately ⅛" from stitched design. Cut out the design just outside the stitching line. Touch the raw edges with gold paint. Allow to dry.

8. Glue the design piece centered onto the box lid.

Thistle Box

Thistle Box

Stitches & Techniques
BULLION-TIPPED LAZY DAISY STITCH
ROLLED STRAIGHT STITCH
STENCILING
STRAIGHT STITCH
TWISTED BULLION-TIPPED LAZY DAISY
   STITCH

Materials
8"-square paper maché box with lid
9" square of ivory fabric; matching thread
6$\frac{1}{2}$" square of cotton batting
3 yards of $\frac{1}{8}$" metallic-gold ribbon
1 yard of $\frac{5}{8}$" flat trim
1mm fuchsia cording
1mm metallic-gold cording
6" embroidery hoop
Disappearing-ink fabric marker
Large-eyed needle (darner)
Scissors
Spray adhesive
Metallic-gold paint
Stencil brush
Checkerboard stencil
Masking tape

Directions
1. Apply gold paint to box using the STENCILING technique (page 19). Allow to dry.

2. Using the SUNLIGHT transfer method (page 13), lightly transfer the design onto the 9" fabric square with the fabric marker. Place the fabric in the embroidery hoop.

3. Stitch the flower petals with STRAIGHT STITCHES (page 16) using fuchsia and metallic-gold cording; stitch the bulb of the flower with BULLION-TIPPED LAZY DAISY STITCHES (page 14).

4. Stitch the stem with ROLLED STRAIGHT STITCHES (page 15) using $\frac{1}{8}$" metallic-gold ribbon. Stitch the leaves with a combination of LAZY DAISY STITCHES and TWISTED BULLION-TIPPED LAZY DAISY STITCHES (pages 15 and 16).

5. Remove the fabric from the hoop. With the design centered, cut fabric to a 6$\frac{1}{2}$" square. Lightly spray the wrong side of the design piece with spray adhesive. With edges aligned, attach the 6$\frac{1}{2}$" square of batting to the design piece; smooth to adhere.

6. Spray the back of the batting with spray adhesive. With design centered, attach the batting/design piece to the top of the box lid.

7. Glue the flat trim and $\frac{1}{8}$" metallic-gold ribbon around the outside edges of the design piece, covering the raw edges.

Thistle Box Pattern

STITCH GUIDE

 Straight Stitch

 Rolled Straight Stitch

 Bullion-Tipped Lazy Daisy

 Twisted Bullion-Tipped Lazy Daisy

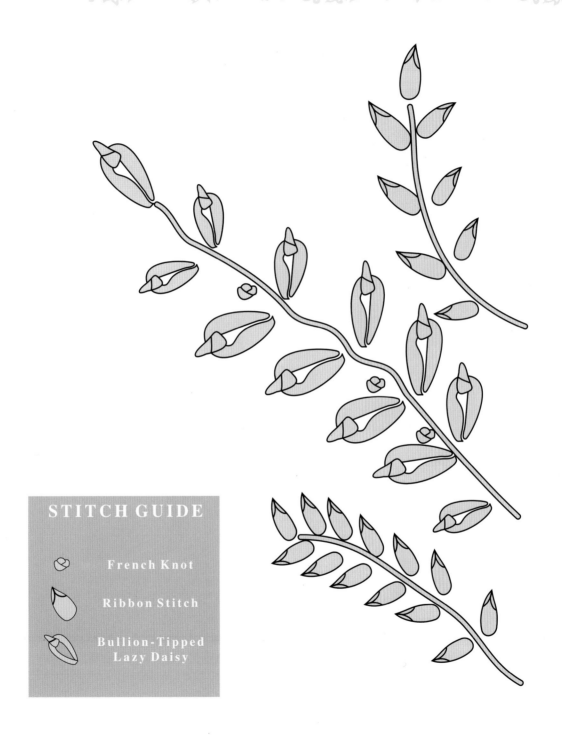

STITCH GUIDE

French Knot

Ribbon Stitch

Bullion-Tipped
Lazy Daisy

Cornucopia

Cornucopia

Stitches & Techniques
BULLION-TIPPED LAZY DAISY STITCH
FRENCH KNOT
RIBBON STITCH
STRAIGHT STITCH

Materials
$1/2$ yard of ivory-and-taupe striped fabric
$1/2$ yard of taupe moiré fabric
7mm ivory textured ribbon
7mm ivory silk ribbon
1.5mm ivory textured ribbon
$1^1/4$ yards of $1/4$" taupe cording
4" taupe tassel
Posterboard
14" embroidery hoop
Disappearing-ink fabric marker
Large-eyed needle (darner)
Scissors
Spray adhesive
Hot glue gun and glue sticks
Craft knife
Straight-edge ruler

Directions
1. From striped fabric, cut one 14" x 14" piece for front. From taupe moiré, cut one front section and two back sections, adding $1/2$" to all edges. From posterboard, cut one front section and two back sections.

2. Using the transfer method of your choice (page 13), lightly transfer the design onto the striped fabric piece with the fabric marker. Place the fabric in the embroidery hoop.

3. Using 1.5mm ivory textured ribbon, stitch STRAIGHT STITCHES (page 16), forming stems. Using 7mm ivory textured ribbon, stitch LAZY DAISY STITCHES (page 15) along center stem, forming leaves. Stitch FRENCH KNOTS (page 14) along stem, using 7mm ivory silk ribbon.

4. Stitch the leaves on the remaining stems with STRAIGHT STITCHES, using 7mm ivory silk ribbon.

5. Remove the fabric from the hoop. With the design centered vertically and the stems aligned with the right side of the front section pattern, cut a front section from the design piece, adding $1/2$" to all edges.

6. Lay ruler along the posterboard front section where scoring is indicated on the pattern. Using the ruler as a guide, partially cut the poster board along the score lines with a craft knife. Do not cut all the way through the posterboard as scoring is intended to weaken the posterboard, making it easier to bend. Lightly spray the scored side of the posterboard front with spray adhesive. Cover with moiré fabric, smoothing out any wrinkles. Cut excess material around edges. Repeat on the opposite side of the posterboard front section, except do not clip edges. Wrap excess edges to the back and hot-glue edges using as little glue as possible. Scrape the glued edges flat with the edge of a hard flat object, such as a credit card. Fold the scored edges to the back.

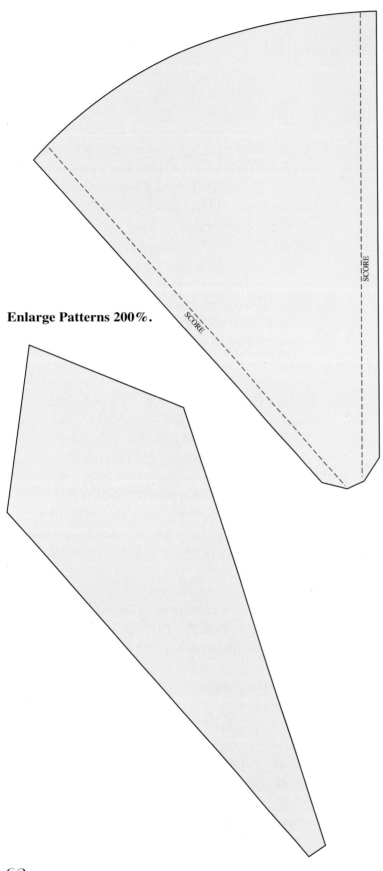

Enlarge Patterns 200%.

SCORE

SCORE

7. Lightly spray one side of one posterboard back section with spray adhesive. Cover with one moiré back section, smoothing out any wrinkles. Repeat on remaining posterboard back section.

8. With right sides up, wrap scored flaps of front section around one back section. Hot-glue flaps to wrong side of back section. Hold in place until glue cools.

9. With wrong sides facing and edges aligned, hot-glue back sections together, sandwiching flaps.

10. Using hot glue sparingly and gluing small sections at a time, glue cording completely around edges of the cornucopia, hiding seams. On inside front edge, glue a small length of cording, covering raw edges. Glue tassel at bottom of cornucopia. Loop a short length of ribbon and glue ends to back of cornucopia,

Luxury & Lace Guest Towels Pattern

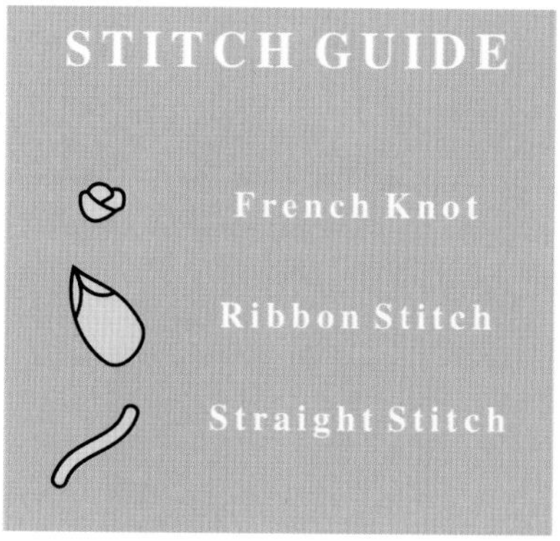

STITCH GUIDE

French Knot

Ribbon Stitch

Straight Stitch

Connect dots to complete pattern.

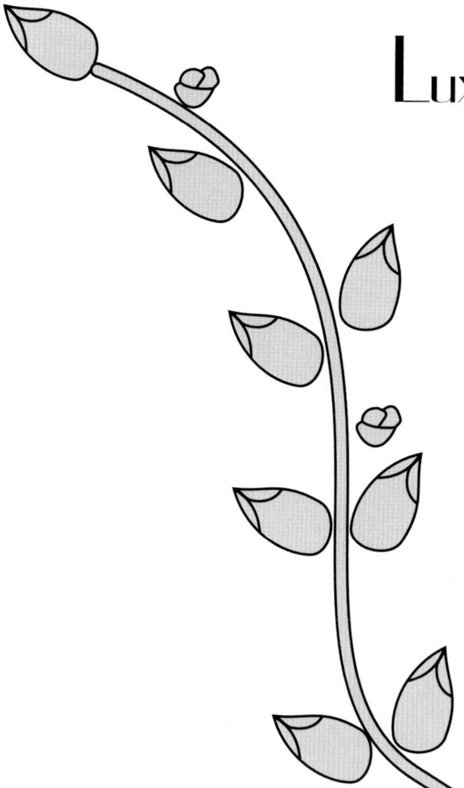

Connect dots to complete pattern.

63

Luxury & Lace Guest Towels

Luxury & Lace Guest Towels

Stitches & Techniques

FRENCH KNOT
RIBBON STITCH
STRAIGHT STITCH

Materials

Two 16" x 30" cotton hand towels
Two 18"-wide crochet or antique lace pieces
2 yards of $1/4$" ivory cording
2 yards of $1/8$" ivory braid
9mm ivory rayon ribbon
Disappearing-ink fabric marker
Large-eyed needle (darner)
Needle and sewing thread
Beading needle
Scissors

Directions

1. Machine- or hand-stitch lace or crochet onto the bottom edge of the towel. Hem side edges if necessary. Hand-stitch $1/4$" ivory cording along stitched edge, covering seam; wrap cut ends to back and tack.

2. Using the transfer method of your choice (page 13), lightly transfer the design onto the flat area at bottom end of the towel with the fabric marker.

3. Stitch the leaves with RIBBON STITCHES (page 15), using 9mm ivory rayon ribbon.

4. Stitch the vine with STRAIGHT STITCHES (page 16), using $1/8$" ivory braid; tack with beading thread to secure.

5. Stitch FRENCH KNOTS (page 14) along vine, using 9mm ivory rayon ribbon.

6. Repeat Steps 1-5 for second towel.

Chamomile Tea Cozy

Chamomile Tea Cozy

Stitches & Techniques
FRENCH KNOT
ROLLED STRAIGHT STITCH
STRAIGHT STITCH

Materials
$1/2$ yard of canvas
$1/2$ yard of muslin
$1/2$ yard of batting
1 yard of 1" gold-edged, white, canvas, wired
    ribbon
7mm white textured ribbon
4mm yellow silk ribbon
1.5mm green textured ribbon
$1/4$" green sheer ribbon
1 yard of $1/4$" fringe trim
1 yard of $1/4$" ivory cording
3" ivory tassel
Gold paint pen
One 10" embroidery hoop
Disappearing-ink fabric marker
Large-eyed needle (darner)
Straight pins
Scissors

Directions
1. From canvas, muslin, and batting, cut two tea cozies each for front and back.

2. Using the transfer method of your choice (page 13), lightly transfer the design onto the front canvas piece with the fabric marker. Place the canvas in the embroidery hoop.

3. Make the flowers by stitching four STRAIGHT STITCHES (page 16) with the 7mm white textured ribbon. Fill in the centers with FRENCH KNOTS (page 14) using 4mm yellow silk ribbon.

4. Stitch long STRAIGHT STITCHES, using 1.5mm green textured ribbon, forming stems. Stitch ROLLED STRAIGHT STITCHES (page 15), using $1/4$" green sheer ribbon, forming leaves.

5. With edges aligned, baste one batting piece to the wrong side of the design piece, $1/2$" from edges. Repeat with remaining canvas and batting pieces.

6. Pin the fringe, with fringed edge toward the center, along the basting line on the right side of the tea cozy front.

7. With right sides facing and edges aligned, stitch the front to the back, sewing along the basting line of the fringe and leaving the bottom edge open. Trim seam; turn.

8. With right sides facing and edges aligned, stitch the lining pieces together, leaving the bottom edge open and a small opening at the top of the seam. Trim seam; do not turn.

9. Slide the lining over the tea cozy, right sides together. Stitch around the bottom edge of the tea cozy. Turn the tea cozy right side out through the opening in the lining. Slip-stitch the opening closed. Stuff the lining inside the tea cozy.

10. Tie a bow with the 1" canvas wired ribbon. Hand-stitch the bow to the tea cozy front over stems. Arrange tails and tack with small stitches to secure. Hand-stitch tassel to top of tea cozy.

11. Using the gold paint pen, write "Chamomile Tea" on tea cozy front.

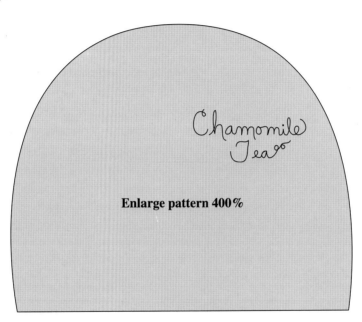

Chamomile Tea

Enlarge pattern 400%

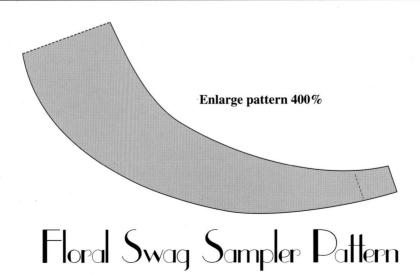

Enlarge pattern 400%

Floral Swag Sampler Pattern

Chamomile Tea Cozy Pattern

STITCH GUIDE

- Rolled Straight Stitch
- French Knot
- Straight Stitch

Floral Swag Sampler

Floral Swag Sampler

Stitches & Techniques
BASIC BUD
FOLDED LEAF
FOLDED AND ROLLED ROSE
MULTIPLE-PETALED FLOWER
STUFFED-RIBBON BERRIES
SINGLE PETAL

Materials
3/4 yard of ivory fabric
3/4 yard of interfacing
Two 2" brass rings
3 yards of 3" sheer gold ribbon
A wide assortment of ribbons, laces, trims and
    buttons
Two purchased artificial-silk leaf sprays
Disappearing-ink fabric marker
Large-eyed needle (darner)
Sewing needle and thread
Scissors
Sewing machine
Craft glue
Hot glue gun and glue sticks

Directions
1. From ivory fabric, cut two swag pieces for front and back. From interfacing, cut one swag piece.

2. Baste interfacing swag piece to the wrong side of one fabric swag piece. With right sides of fabric swag pieces facing and edges aligned, machine-stitch together with a 5/8" seam and leaving a 4" opening for turning.

3. Trim seams and clip curves. Turn right side out through opening. Slip stitch opening closed. Press.

4. Fold each end 2" over a brass ring and stitch to secure.

5. Cut the 3 yards of 3" sheer gold ribbon into two equal lengths. Make two bows and stitch them to each end next to the brass rings on the front of the swag.

6. From the assorted ribbons, laces and trims, make an approximately 10 BASIC BUDS, 30 FOLDED LEAVES, 20 FOLDED AND ROLLED ROSES, 10 MULTIPLE-PETALED FLOWERS, AND 20 STUFFED-RIBBON BERRIES (pages 17 and 18).

7. Arrange all the flowers, leaves, and buttons onto the front of the swag as desired and tack in place with stitches. (Items may be hot-glued in place if desired.)

Embellished Blazer

Embellished Blazer

Stitches & Techniques
BASIC BUD
BULLION-TIPPED LAZY DAISY STITCH
FOLDED LEAF
LAZY DAISY STITCH
MULTIPLE-PETALED ROSE
RIBBON STITCH
SATIN STITCH
SINGLE PETAL
WRAPPED BUD

Materials
Vintage men's tuxedo or jacket
13" of 1³/₄" antique lace
12¹/₂" length of 1¹/₄" antique lace
12¹/₂" length of 2" antique lace
2¹/₄ yards of 1" plum velvet ribbon
12¹/₂" length of 1¹/₂" brown sheer, gold-accent
    ribbon
12¹/₂" length of 1¹/₂" tan velvet ribbon
16" length of brown velvet ribbon
12¹/₂" length of 1¹/₂" bronze sheer, gold-accent
    ribbon
8" length of 1¹/₂" green fancy ribbon
8" length of 1" green velvet ribbon
7mm green sheer, gold-edged ribbon
7mm green sheer ribbon
Disappearing-white-ink fabric marker
Quilting needle and thread
Large embroidery needle
Scissors

Directions
1. To make the large roses, cut 1" brown velvet
    ribbon into four 4" lengths. Overlap the
    ends of one 4" length, forming a point; see
    diagram. Just right of the point, begin
    rolling the ribbon toward the left, forming
    bud; see diagram. Stitch to secure. Run a
    gathering stitch along three edges of each of
    the remaining 1¹/₂" tan velvet ribbon
    lengths. Pull gathers tight, forming three
    1¹/₄" SINGLE PETALS (page 17); knot
    thread to secure. Wrap each petal around the
    bud, slightly overlapping each petal; see
    diagram. Stitch to secure. Repeat to make
    two flowers from 1" plum velvet ribbon.

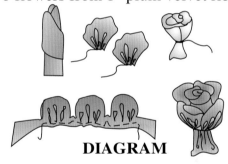

DIAGRAM

2. To make the outer multiple petal sections,
    mark each of the five 12¹/₂" lengths of
    ribbon or lace at 4" intervals, beginning and
    ending ¹/₄" from ends. Stitch a hand-
    gathering stitch following the basic instruc-
    tions for making a MULTIPLE-PETALED
    FLOWER (page 17). Pull gathers tight; knot
    thread to secure. Wrap two gathered lengths
    around each flower, slightly overlapping
    each length (except the brown flower which
    has only one gathered length).

3. Using the transfer method of your choice
    (page 13), lightly transfer the basic design
    of the rosebud, stems and leaves onto the
    jacket lapels with fabric marker.

4. Make a BASIC BUD (page 17) with a 4" length of 1" plum velvet ribbon. Repeat to make seven buds. With a 4" length of 1" green velvet ribbon, make a WRAPPED BUD (page 18).

5. Lay the buds in place on the jacket, tacking the unfinished bottom half of the buds securely onto the fabric with quilting thread. Cover the unfinished areas with SATIN STITCHES (page 15), using 7mm green sheer ribbon; continue SATIN STITCHES to form the stem.

6. Stitch four loose RIBBON STITCHES (page 15) over the base of each bud, forming the calyx; see photo. Stitch LAZY DAISY STITCHES (page 15) with 7mm green sheer, gold-edged ribbon along the stem, forming leaves.

7. Make three FOLDED LEAVES (page 17) with 4" lengths of 1" green velvet and 1$^{1}/_{2}$" green fancy ribbon.

8. Hand-stitch leaves and large flowers to the lapel. Stitch BULLION-TIPPED LAZY DAISY STITCHES (page 14) using 7mm green sheer ribbon.

9. Hand-stitch remaining length of antique lace under the upper collar section of the jacket.

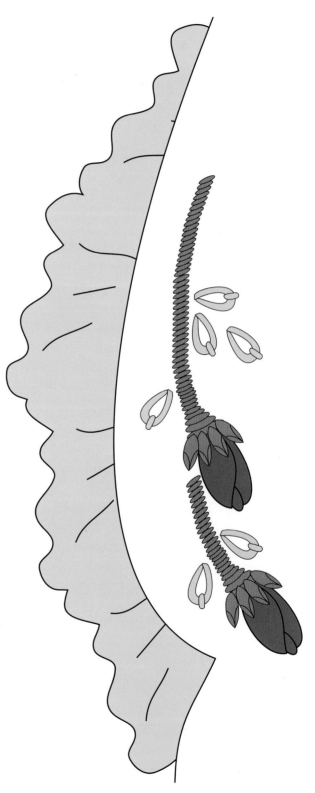

Embellished Blazer Pattern

STITCH GUIDE

Lazy Daisy
Stitch

Straight Stitch

Bullion-Tipped
Lazy Daisy

Ribbon Stitch

Victorian Hat

Victorian Hat

Stitches & Techniques
BASIC BUD
FOLDED LEAF
LAZY DAISY STITCH
MULTIPLE-PETALED ROSE
SINGLE PETAL
STUFFED-RIBBON BERRIES

Materials
Purchased brown velvet hat
4" x 5" piece of antique lace
16" length of $1^1/_2$" tan velvet ribbon
13" of 1" plum velvet ribbon
$12^1/_2$" length of $1^1/_2$" brown velvet ribbon
$12^1/_2$" length of $1^1/_2$" brown sheer, gold-accent ribbon
$12^1/_2$" length of 2" metallic-gold trim
7mm green sheer, gold-edged ribbon
4" length of $1^1/_2$" green fancy ribbon
4" length of 1" green velvet ribbon
$1^1/_2$ yards of $2^1/_2$" bronze ribbon
Small amount of stuffing
Disappearing-white-ink fabric marker
Large-eyed needle (darner)
Quilting needle and thread

Directions
1. To make the large rose, cut $1^1/_2$" tan velvet ribbon into four 4" lengths. Overlap the ends of one 4" length, forming a point; see diagram. Just right of the point, begin rolling the ribbon toward the left, forming bud; see diagram. Stitch to secure. Run a gathering stitch along the short ends and one long edge of each of the remaining $1^1/_2$" tan velvet ribbon lengths. Pull gathers tight, forming three $1^1/_4$" SINGLE PETALS (page 17; knot thread to secure. Wrap each petal around the bud, slightly overlapping each petal; see diagram. Stitch to secure.

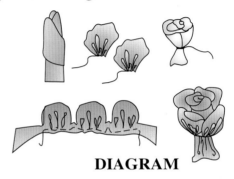

DIAGRAM

2. To make the outer multiple petal sections, mark each $12^1/_2$" length of ribbon at 4" intervals, beginning and ending $1/_4$" from ends. Stitch a hand-gathering stitch following the basic instructions for making a MULTIPLE- PETALED FLOWER (page 17). Pull gathers tight; knot thread to secure. Wrap each gathered length around flower, slightly overlapping each length.

3. Run a gathering stitch along one edge of the 4" x 5" piece of antique lace. Pull gathers; knot thread to secure.

4. Make a FOLDED LEAF (page 17) with 4" length of green fancy ribbon.

5. Make a BASIC BUD (page 17) with 4" length of 1" plum velvet and 4" length of 1" green velvet ribbon.

6. Make three STUFFED-RIBBON BERRIES (page 18) with three 3" lengths of 1" plum velvet ribbon.

7. Wrap the 1½ yard length of 2½" bronze ribbon around the brim of the hat, tying ends into a 6" bow. Hand-tack to secure. Arrange flowers, bud, berries, lace, and leaf as shown in photo or as desired. Hand-stitch or hot-glue items in place to secure.

8. Using the LAZY DAISY STITCH (page 15) with 7mm green sheer, gold-edged ribbon, stitch three clusters of leaves as shown in photo or as desired.

STITCH GUIDE

Lazy Daisy Stitch

Stuffed-Ribbon Berries

Roses Throw Pillow Pattern

STITCH GUIDE

╱	Straight Stitch
✓	Lazy Daisy Stitch
●	French Knot
✓	Feather Stitch
✳	Wave Stitch

Roses Throw Pillow

Roses Throw Pillow

Stitches & Techniques
FEATHER STITCH
FRENCH KNOT
LAZY DAISY STITCH
STRAIGHT STITCH
WAVE STITCH

Materials
14" purchased taupe throw pillow
$^5/_8$" gold rayon ribbon
4mm gold silk ribbon
$2^1/_4$ yards of 1" ivory sheer ribbon
Taupe embroidery floss
Disappearing-ink fabric marker
Large-eyed needle (darner)
Scissors

Directions
1. Using the transfer method of your choice (page 13), lightly transfer the design onto the pillow front with the fabric marker.

2. Stitch leaves with LAZY DAISY STITCHES (page 15), using $^5/_8$" gold rayon ribbon. Stitch branches with FEATHER STITCHES (page 14), using 4mm gold silk ribbon.

3. Stitch the spoke design with embroidery floss. Cut a 27" length of 1" ivory sheer ribbon. Tack the end to the center of the spoke design with embroidery floss. Work the WAVE STITCH (page 16) around the first row of spokes, gradually looping fuller looped rows as you work outward. When you have completed each row of loops, thread the ribbon back inside the loops to the center. Tack the end under a loop, covering raw edges. Repeat to make three flowers.

4. Stitch loose FRENCH KNOTS (page 14) at the center of each flower, using 4mm gold silk ribbon.

Heirloom Pin Bookmark

Wedding Rose & Heirloom Pin Bookmarks

Stitches & Techniques
FOLDED AND ROLLED ROSE
SINGLE PETAL

Materials
$1/2$ yard of $1/2$" ivory sheer, picot-edged ribbon
14" length of $1^5/8$"ivory embroidered trim
11" length of 1" ivory sheer, silk-edged ribbon
One 3" ivory tassel
Quilting needle and thread
Large-eyed needle (darner)
Scissors

Directions
Photo on page 4.
1. Make a FOLDED AND ROLLED ROSE (page 17) from the 11" length of 1" ivory sheer, silk-edged ribbon.

2. Cut the $1/2$ yard length of $1/2$" ivory sheer, picot-edged ribbon into three 6" lengths. Make three SINGLE PETALS (page 17). Wrap the gathered edge of one petal around the base of the rose; hand-stitch to secure. Repeat, slightly overlapping each petal.

3. Fold the top edge of the 14" length of $1^5/8$" ivory embroidered trim down $1/4$"; fold again 2" down and hand-hem-stitch to secure.

4. Fold the bottom edge of the ribbon into a point and hand-stitch to secure. Stitch tassel to the point.

Stitches & Techniques
FOLDED LEAF

Materials
12" length of $1^1/2$"green textured ribbon
One vintage floral pendant
7" length of 1" green velvet ribbon
$1/4$ yard of 1" green pleated ribbon
One 3" gold tassel
Quilting thread
Large-eyed needle (darner)

Directions
1. Cut two $3^1/2$" lengths from the 1" green velvet ribbon. Make two FOLDED LEAVES (page 17).

2. Double-fold the top edge of the 12" length of $1^1/2$"green textured ribbon $1/4$" and hand-hem-stitch to secure.

3. Fold the bottom edge of the ribbon into a point and hand-stitch to secure. Stitch tassel to the point.

4. Attach the pendant to the top of the ribbon with its pin or with hot glue.

5. Run a hand-gathering stitch along one edge of the 1" green pleated ribbon; pull the gathers tightly, forming a fan shape. Arrange the pleated fan around the pendant, allowing it to extend approximately $1/4$" beyond the outer pendant edge; hand-stitch in place, tacking one folded leaf in front and one behind the pleated fan.

Flanged Pillow Cover, Bed Shawl
& Linens with Lace

Flanged Pillow Cover

Stitches & Techniques
BEAD COUCHING
FOLDED AND ROLLED ROSE
FRENCH KNOT
LAZY DAISY STITCH
STACKED FLY STITCH

Materials
1 yard of flax fabric
$1/4$ yard of netting
$5/8$" gold rayon ribbon
$5/8$" ivory/gold sheer ribbon
4mm gold silk ribbon
Assorted gold seed beads
14"-diameter embroidery hoop
Disappearing-ink fabric marker
Large-eyed needle (darner)
Beading needle and thread
Straight pins
Scissors

Directions
All seams are $5/8$".

1. From flax fabric, cut one 30" x 26" piece for pillow front and two 18" x 26" pieces for pillow backs. Using the NETTING transfer method (page 13), transfer the design onto the pillow front. Place the pillow front in the embroidery hoop.

2. Layer two 30" lengths of $5/8$" gold rayon ribbon together and tie into a 9" bow. Arrange the bow at the base of the design and secure in place with straight pins. Tack the bow and tails by BEAD COUCHING (page 14) seed beads to the ribbon bow and tails with beading floss.

3. Stitch the "U"-shaped design area with STACKED FLY STITCHES (page 16), using 4mm gold silk ribbon. Begin each leaf with an irregular-shaped fly stitch to give the appearance of a curved leaf.

4. Fill the lower portion of the design with LAZY DAISY STITCHES (page 15), using $5/8$" ivory/gold sheer ribbon. Also stitch FRENCH KNOTS (page 14).

5. Make two FOLDED AND ROLLED ROSES (page 17) from $5/8$" gold rayon ribbon and one from $5/8$" gold/ivory sheer ribbon. Hand-stitch roses to the center of the bow.

6. Fold one long edge of one pillow back piece under $1/4$"; double-fold edge under 1" and press. Hem folded edge. Repeat on remaining pillow back piece.

7. With right sides facing, pin pillow front to backs with raw edges aligned and hemmed edges overlapping in the center.

8. Stitch $5/8$" seams completely around pillow edges. Clip corners. Turn right side out. Press.

9. Topstitch around pillow $3^1/2$" inside finished edge.

STITCH GUIDE

Bead Couching

Folded & Rolled Rose

French Knot

Stacked Fly Stitch

Lazy Daisy Stitch

Flanged Pillow Cover Pattern

Monogrammed Throw Pillow

Monogrammed Throw Pillow & Bed Shawl

Stitches & Techniques
SATIN STITCH

Materials
One 14"-square purchased throw pillow
7mm ivory silk ribbon
Four 4" taupe tassels
Disappearing-ink fabric marker
Large-eyed needle (darner)
Needle and sewing thread
Scissors

Directions
1. Stitch one tassel to each corner of the pillow.

2. Using the transfer method of your choice (page 13), lightly transfer the monogram onto the pillow front with the fabric marker.

3. Stitch the entire monogram with SATIN STITCHES (page 15), using 7mm ivory silk ribbon. Avoid twisting the ribbon and keep the stitches fairly loose.

4. Hide the ends of the ribbon by taking a long stitch away from the design; then bring the needle up through the fabric and cut it off very close to the fabric.

Stitches & Techniques
BEAD COUCHING
FOLDED AND ROLLED ROSE

Materials
One 38"-square, fringed, shawl
5 yards of $5/8$" gold rayon ribbon
1 yard of $5/8$" ivory/gold sheer ribbon
Assorted gold seed beads
Large-eyed needle (darner)
Beading needle and thread
Straight pins
Scissors

Directions
1. Cut a 1 yard length of $5/8$" gold rayon ribbon; set aside. Make a three-looped bow at the center of the remaining $5/8$" gold rayon ribbon.

2. Arrange the tails of the bow, looping and folding along the sides of the shawl; pin in place to secure.

3. Tack the ribbon by BEAD COUCHING (page 14) seed beads at 1" intervals along the bow and tails.

4. Make eight FOLDED AND ROLLED ROSES (page 17) from the 1 yard lengths of $5/8$" gold rayon and $5/8$" ivory/gold sheer ribbons. Tack the roses at the center of the bow and along tails, as shown in photo.

A B C D E

F G H I J

K L M N O

P 2 R S T U

V W X Y Z

Linens with Lace

Stitches & Techniques
BEAD COUCHING
FOLDED AND ROLLED ROSE

Materials
One flat twin sheet
2"-wide lace, width of sheet
56" length of ⅝" gold rayon ribbon
9" length of ⅝" ivory/gold sheer ribbon
Assorted gold seed beads
Large-eyed needle (darner)
Beading needle and thread
Needle and sewing thread
Straight pins
Scissors

Directions

1. Machine- or hand-stitch lace across the top edge of the sheet. Hem side edges if necessary.

2. Tie a 5" bow at the center of the 56" length of ⅝" gold rayon ribbon.

3. Center the bow on the lace-covered edge of the sheet. Knot each of the bow tails at 3" intervals. Arrange the tails and pin in place to secure.

4. Tack the ribbon by BEAD COUCHING (page 14) seed beads at 1" intervals along the tails.

5. Make a FOLDED AND ROLLED ROSE (page 17) from the 9" length of ⅝" ivory/gold sheer ribbon. Tack the rose at the center of the bow.

Decorative Soap Bag

Decorative Soap Bag

Stitches & Techniques
CASCADING
FRENCH KNOT
LAZY DAISY STITCH

Materials
Two 9" x 7" pieces of sheer fabric
28" length of ³/₄" gold sheer ribbon
4mm gold silk ribbon
4mm green silk ribbon
Disappearing-ink fabric marker
Large-eyed needle (darner)
Sewing machine
Scissors

Directions
1. Using the the transfer method of your choice (page 13), lightly transfer the design onto one piece of fabric with the fabric marker.

2. Using the LAZY DAISY STITCH (page 15) with 4mm gold silk ribbon, stitch leaf sprays up both sides of the design. Stitch FRENCH KNOTS (page 14) above and around the leaf sprays.

3. Stitch the bow at the center of the design, using large LAZY DAISY STITCHES (page 15) with 4mm green silk ribbon. Then, CASCADE (page 14) the tails of the bow using 4mm green silk ribbon.

4. With right sides facing and edges aligned, stitch the fabric pieces together, leaving the top edge unstitched.

5. Turn the bag right side out and press seams.

6. Fill the bag with small soaps and tie the top edge with the 28" length of gold sheer ribbon.

Herbed Bottle

Herbed Bottle

Stitches & techniques

FRENCH KNOT
LAZY DAISY STITCH

Materials

One 12" decorative bottle
36" length of 2" olive-green sheer ribbon
12" length of 3" antique flat lace
4mm olive-green silk ribbon
4mm sage-green silk ribbon
Disappearing-ink fabric marker
Large-eyed needle (darner)
Straight pins
Scissors

Directions

1. Wrap the decorative bottle with the antique lace so that it fits smoothly around the center of the bottle. Fold the raw ends under so that they overlap slightly. Hand-stitch to secure.

2. Tie the 2" olive-green sheer ribbon around the bottle just above the lace and tie a 5" bow. Place a straight pin through the bow to keep the knot from coming untied while stitching.

3. Using the transfer method of your choice (page 13), lightly transfer the design onto the tails of the bow with the fabric marker. Cut the ends of the tails at a diagonal.

4. Using the LAZY DAISY STITCH (page 15) with 4mm olive-green silk ribbon, stitch leaf sprays on both bow tails. Using 4mm sage-green silk ribbon, stitch FRENCH KNOTS (page 14) around the leaf sprays.

5. Remove the pin from the bow knot and stitch a cluster of FRENCH KNOTS at the center of the bow, using 4mm sage-green silk ribbon.

STITCH GUIDE

🌀 French Knot

Cascading

Lazy Daisy Stitch

Decorative Soap Bag Pattern

STITCH GUIDE

Lazy Daisy Stitch

French Knot

Herbed Bottle Pattern

96

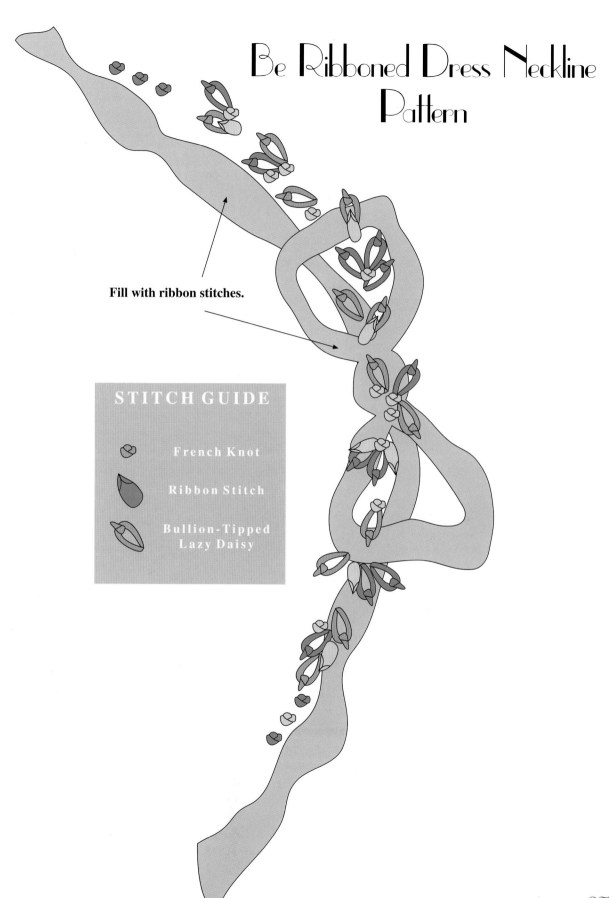

Be Ribboned Dress Neckline Pattern

Fill with ribbon stitches.

STITCH GUIDE

French Knot

Ribbon Stitch

Bullion-Tipped
Lazy Daisy

Be Ribboned Dress Neckline

Be Ribboned Dress Neckline

Stitches & Techniques

BULLION-TIPPED LAZY DAISY STITCH
FRENCH KNOT
RIBBON STITCH

Materials

One dress with scooped neckline
4mm rose silk ribbon
4mm dark-rose silk ribbon
4mm green silk ribbon
4mm light-green silk ribbon
Disappearing-ink fabric marker
Large-eyed needle (darner)
Scissors

Directions

1. Using the transfer method of your choice (page 13), lightly transfer the design onto the neckline of the dress with the fabric marker.

2. Fill the entire bow area with side by side RIBBON STITCHES (page 15), using 4mm medium-rose silk ribbon.

3. Stitch the leaves with BULLION-TIPPED LAZY DAISY STITCHES (page 14), using 4mm green silk ribbon; also stitch the buds with BULLION-TIPPED LAZY DAISY STITCHES, using 4mm rose silk ribbon

4. Stitch RIBBON STITCHES with 4mm light-green silk ribbon around the leaves and buds. Using 4mm green silk ribbon and 4mm dark-rose silk ribbon, stitch FRENCH KNOTS (page 14) around the design.

Vintage Book Display

Vintage Book Display

Stitches & Techniques
FOLDED LEAF
STUFFED-RIBBON BERRIES

Materials
One vintage book
2 yards of 2" green sheer ribbon
$1/2$ yard of 1" ivory sheer ribbon
$1/2$ yard of $1/2$" ivory striped ribbon
$1/4$ yard of 1" green sheer ribbon
7" length of $3/4$" teal ribbon
2" circle of buckram
Small amount of stuffing
Large-eyed needle (darner)
Needle and gold thread
Three 1" artificial stamens
$1/2$" white decorative button
$1^1/2$" pin back
Scissors
Hot glue gun and glue sticks

Directions
1. Cut all ivory ribbons into 3" lengths. Make twelve FOLDED LEAVES (page 17).

2. Arrange the FOLDED LEAVES into two six-petaled flowers.

3. Stitch the smaller flower over the larger one. Stitch the button in the center.

4. Make three STUFFED-RIBBON BERRIES (page 18) with three $2^1/3$" lengths of $3/4$" teal ribbon. Stitch a short length of gold thread onto the center of each berry. Knot free ends of the threads together so that the berries dangle about an 1" to $1^1/2$" apart.

5. Arrange the flowers, berries, stamens, and leaves and hot-glue onto the buckram circle; see photo. Hot-glue the pin back to the back of the circle.

6. Tie a 6" bow around the book with the 2" sheer ribbon. Pin the ribbon arrangement over the center of the bow.

Ribbon Hair Bow

Ribbon Hair Bow

Stitches & Techniques
BASIC BUD
FOLDED LEAF
MULTIPLE PETAL
STUFFED-RIBBON BERRIES
SINGLE PETAL
WRAPPED BUD

Materials
One 3" hair clip
1 yard of $1^{1}/4$" green velvet ribbon
$27^{1}/2$" length of $1^{1}/4$" apricot velvet ribbon
6" length of $1^{1}/4$" green tapestry ribbon
4" length of 1" gold, black-edged ribbon
Small amount of stuffing
Large-eyed needle (darner)
Needle and heavy-duty sewing thread
Three 1" artificial stamens
Scissors
Hot glue gun and glue sticks

Directions

1. Cut the green velvet ribbon into two 14" lengths. Overlap the ends of one length, forming a $5^{1}/2$" rectangle. Repeat for the second length, forming a $4^{1}/2$" rectangle. Lay the smaller rectangle over the larger one and tie them together at the center with thread, forming a bow; see photo.

2. Cut the apricot velvet ribbon into six 3" lengths and one $9^{1}/2$" length. From the 3" lengths, make five SINGLE PETALS (page 17) and one BASIC BUD (page 17). Beginning and ending $^{1}/4$" from ends, mark scallops at 3" intervals on the $9^{1}/2$" length of apricot velvet ribbon. Make a MULTIPLE PETAL section (page 17).

3. Wrap the remining green velvet ribbon around the apricot bud, forming a WRAPPED BUD (page 18).

4. Make a STUFFED-RIBBON BERRY (page 18) with gold, black-edged ribbon. Stitch a 2" length of gold thread onto the center of the berry.

5. Make two FOLDED LEAVES (page 17) from the green tapestry ribbon.

6. Wrap each of the five petals around the cluster of three stamens, overlapping each petal and securing with stitches at the bottom gathered edge. Wrap the multiple petal piece around the flower; secure with stitches

7. Arrange the flower, leaves and berry on the center of the bow and hot-glue; see photo. Hot-glue the hair clip to the back of the bow.

It is amazing how many fun things you can do to personalize and embellish your frames and mats, once you simply remove the glass from the frame and enter the third dimension.

Embellished Picture Frames

Embellished Oval Mat with Leaves

Stitches & Techniques
FOLDED LEAF

Materials
One framed photo with oval mat (glass removed)
One 1$\frac{1}{2}$" resin rose
6" length of 1$\frac{1}{4}$" sheer, decorative ribbon
$\frac{1}{2}$ yard of silver 1" ribbon
$\frac{1}{2}$ yard of ivory 1" ribbon
12" of $\frac{1}{2}$" ivory striped ribbon
A length of $\frac{1}{2}$" trim equal to the measurement
   of the four inside edges of the frame plus 1"
Needle and sewing thread
Scissors
Hot glue gun and glue sticks
Wax metallic-gold finish
Liquid gold leaf
Cotton swab
Scrap rags

Directions
1. Using a scrap rag, rub the wax metallic-gold finish around the outside edges of the frame, highlighting any embossed areas.

2. Using a cotton swab, apply the liquid gold leaf to the resin flower. Let dry.

3. Cut all ribbons into 3" lengths; make 18 FOLDED LEAVES (page 17).

4. Hot-glue the $\frac{1}{2}$" trim around the outside edge of the mat.

5. Hot-glue the leaves around the mat at the top of the oval and glue the resin rose in the center; see photo.

Bow & Leaf Embellished Frames

Stitches & Techniques
FOLDED AND ROLLED ROSE

Materials
One framed photo with mat (glass removed)
1½ yards of 1" beige/gold wire-edged canvas
    ribbon
Needle and sewing thread
Scissors
Hot glue gun and glue sticks
Wax metallic-gold finish
Scrap rags

Directions
1. Using a scrap rag, rub the wax metallic-gold finish around the outside edges of the frame.

2. Cut an 11" length from the 1" beige/gold wire-edged canvas ribbon; set aside. Tie remaining ribbon into a bow and hot-glue it to the center top edge of the mat. Arrange the tails of the bow and glue them to the mat; see photo.

3. From the 11" length of 1" beige/gold wire-edged canvas ribbon, make a FOLDED AND ROLLED ROSE (page 17). Hot-glue the rose to the center of the bow.

Stitches & Techniques
FOLDED LEAF
STUFFED-RIBBON BERRIES

Materials
One framed photo with mat (glass removed)
½ yard of 1¼" green ribbon
Thirteen 3" lengths of assorted ribbon
Small amount of stuffing
Needle and sewing thread
Scissors
Hot glue gun and glue sticks

Directions
1. From the assorted 3" lengths of ribbon, make ten FOLDED LEAVES (page 17) and three STUFFED-RIBBON BERRIES (page 18).

2. Hot-glue the length of 1¼" green ribbon up the left edge of the frame, twisting and turning the ribbon as you tack it down with hot glue.

3. Arrange and hot-glue the leaves and berries to the frame; see photo.

Natural Beauty Sweater

Natural Beauty Sweater

Stitches & Techniques
BEAD COUCHING
FOLDED AND ROLLED ROSE
FRENCH KNOT
LAZY DAISY STITCH
SPIDER WEB ROSE

Materials
One purchased sweater with scoop neckline
1/8" gold cording
12"-square of netting
7mm taupe heirloom sylk ribbon
7mm green heirloom sylk ribbon
7mm rust heirloom sylk ribbon
4mm amber heirloom sylk ribbon
Rust seed beads
Disappearing-ink fabric marker
Large-eyed needle (darner)
Beading needle and floss
Scissors

Directions

1. Using the NETTING transfer method (page 13), lightly transfer the design onto the neckline on the front and back of the sweater with the fabric marker.

2. Lay the gold cording on the sweater, forming the vine; BEAD COUCH (page 14) the cording in place with beading floss and seed beads. Using LAZY DAISY STITCHES (page 15), stitch the leaves with the 7mm green heirloom sylk ribbon. Stitch FRENCH KNOTS (page 14) with 4mm amber heirloom sylk ribbon.

3. Using 7mm rust and 7mm taupe heirloom sylk ribbons, make FOLDED AND ROLLED ROSES (page 17); tack into place with beading floss.

4. Using 7mm taupe heirloom sylk ribbon, stitch SPIDER WEB ROSES (page 15). Stitch FRENCH KNOTS at the center of some roses with 4mm amber heirloom sylk ribbon.

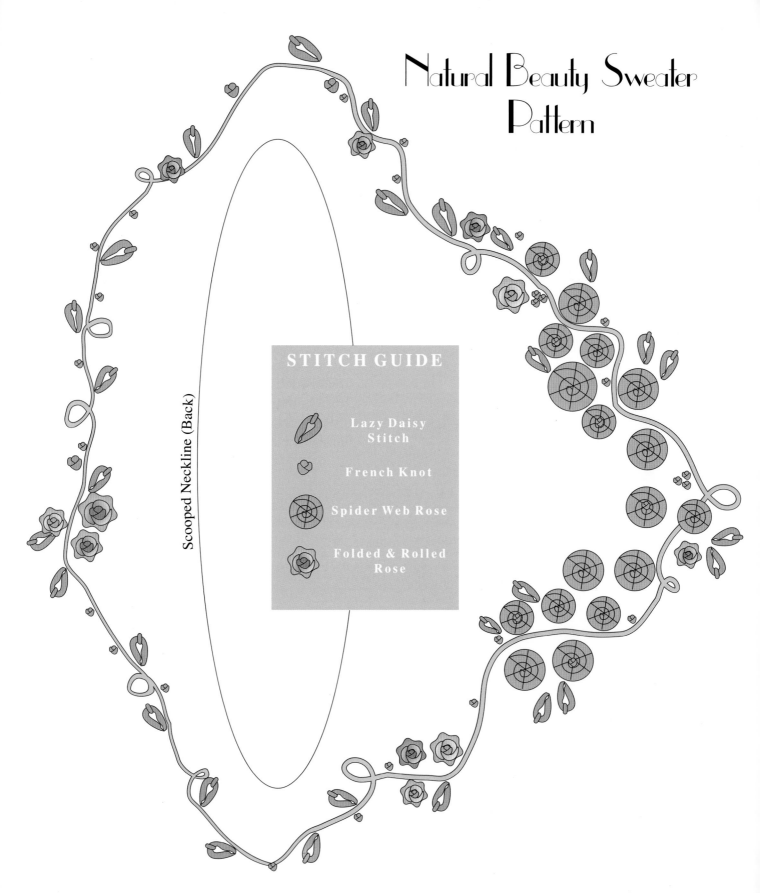

Natural Beauty Sweater
Pattern

Scooped Neckline (Back)

STITCH GUIDE

Lazy Daisy
Stitch

French Knot

Spider Web Rose

Folded & Rolled
Rose

Woodland Frame

Woodland Frame

Stitches & Techniques
BULLION-TIPPED LAZY DAISY STITCH
FOLDED AND ROLLED ROSE
FRENCH KNOT
LAZY DAISY STITCH

Materials
5" x 7" picture-frame mat with oval opening
Two 5" x 7" pieces of mat board
$1/4$ yard of ivory fabric
$1/4$ yard of bonded batting
$1^1/4$" silver bird charm
Small twigs
Gray spanish moss
$1^1/4$ yard of $1/2$" ivory decorative trim
$1^1/4$ yard of $1/4$" ivory cording
4mm gray/green silk ribbon
4mm textured gray/green ribbon
7mm textured gray/green ribbon
Disappearing-ink fabric marker
Large-eyed needle (darner)
Scissors
Craft glue
Hot glue gun and glue sticks
Picture hanger

Directions
1. Using the 5" x 7" picture-frame mat with oval opening as a pattern, cut two pieces from batting (cut one $1/4$" larger on all edges). Also, trace the outside and inside edges of the pattern onto the fabric with an erasable marker. Then, using the transfer method of your choice (page 13), lightly transfer the design onto the fabric with the fabric marker.

2. Stitch leaves using the LAZY DAISY STITCH (page 15) with 4mm gray/green silk ribbon. Stitch BULLION-TIPPED LAZY DAISY STITCHES (page 14) with 4mm gray/green textured ribbon. Stitch FRENCH KNOTS (page 14) with 4mm gray/green silk ribbon.

3. Cut the fabric $3/4$" beyond picture-frame-mat tracing lines.

4. Make three FOLDED AND ROLLED ROSES (page 17) from 7mm gray/green textured ribbon. Set aside.

5. Spray the backs of the batting pieces with spray adhesive. Place the smaller piece on the picture-frame mat with oval opening. Place the larger batting piece on the smaller one. Spray the top of the batting/mat with spray adhesive; then, lay the stitched piece, right side up, on the batting/mat. Clip the overlapping edges of the fabric inside the oval at $3/8$" intervals, stopping $1/4$" from the edge of the mat. Fold the fabric around to the back side and hot-glue in place.

6. Trim the corner edges diagonally $3/8$" from the edge of the mat; fold to the back and hot-glue. Fold and glue the outer edges to back. Repeat to cover the two 5" x 7" pieces of mat board for backs.

7. With wrong sides facing, glue the two backs together. Hot-glue the front to the back along bottom and side edges, leaving the top edge open to insert photo.

8. Hot-glue the ribbon roses, bird charm, sticks, and moss on the frame front; see photo.

9. Glue the ¼" ivory cording around the outside edge of the frame. Glue the ½" ivory decorative trim around the inside oval and around outer edges of the frame back. Glue a hanger to the back side of the frame.

STITCH GUIDE

Lazy Daisy Stitch

Bullion-Tipped Lazy Daisy

French Knot

Folded & Rolled Rose

Spring Wreath

Spring Wreath

Stitches & Techniques
FRENCH KNOT
RIBBON STITCH
STRAIGHT STITCH

Materials
Picture frame with a 6" x 7¹/₂" window
6¹/₂" x 8" piece of mat board
5" x 6" piece of lightweight cotton fabric
5" x 6" piece of fusible webbing
51" of beige cording
³/₄" lovebirds charm
³/₈" plastic button
7mm taupe heirloom sylk ribbon
4mm dark-green heirloom sylk ribbon
4mm light-green heirloom sylk ribbon
4mm lavender heirloom sylk ribbon
4mm purple heirloom sylk ribbon
4mm dark-purple heirloom sylk ribbon
2mm brown trim
1mm green cording
Disappearing-ink fabric marker
Large-eyed needle (darner)
Beading needle and floss
Scissors
Craft glue
Color photocopy machine

Directions
1. Cut the 7mm taupe heirloom sylk ribbon into 6" strips. Place the strips side by side onto fusible webbing. Fuse the ribbon strips onto cotton fabric piece following manufacturer's instructions, forming door area.

2. Using the transfer method of your choice (page 13), lightly transfer the design onto the fabric with the fabric marker.

3. Cut the 51" of beige cording into three equal lengths. Braid lengths together. Stitch the ends together, forming a 2" circle, and trim the excess cording. Center and hand-stitch circle to door area.

4. Using STRAIGHT STITCHES (page 16), make the stem and branches with the 2mm brown trim. Tack the stitches in place with beading thread, creating the look of a vine climbing up the stem to the wreath.

5. Using RIBBON STITCHES (page 15), make the leaves with 4mm dark-green and light-green heirloom sylk ribbon. Stitch FRENCH KNOTS,(page 14) to make the buds with 4mm lavender, purple and dark-purple heirloom sylk ribbon.

6. Glue the lovebirds charm to the bottom center of the wreath.

7. Photocopy pattern onto mat board. Cut out opening and place over stitching. Place in frame.

STITCH GUIDE

Ribbon Stitch

French Knot

Straight Stitch

Summer Wreath

Summer Wreath

Stitches & Techniques
CASCADING
FRENCH KNOTS
RIBBON STITCH
TWO-STITCH TWISTED ROSE

Materials
Picture frame with a 6" x 7½" window
6½" x 8" piece of mat board
5" x 6" piece of lightweight cotton fabric
5" x 6" piece of fusible webbing
½" glass button
Two ³⁄₈" brass heart charms
48" of ⅝" tan velvet ribbon
4mm light-rose heirloom sylk ribbon
4mm medium-rose heirloom sylk ribbon
4mm dark-rose heirloom sylk ribbon
4mm light-green heirloom sylk ribbon
3mm brown rayon ribbon
Disappearing-ink fabric marker
Large-eyed needle (darner)
Beading needle and floss
Scissors
Craft glue
Color photocopy machine

Directions
1. Cut the 48" of ⅝" tan velvet ribbon into 6" strips. Place the strips side by side onto fusible webbing. Fuse the ribbon strips onto cotton fabric piece following manufacturer's instructions, forming door area.

2. Using the transfer method of your choice (page 13), lightly transfer the design onto the fabric with the fabric marker.

3. CASCADE (page 14) the 3mm brown rayon ribbon around the heart shape to create the grapevine wreath. Take a few backstitches at the bottom point of the heart; cut the ribbon at ³⁄₄" lengths, creating vine ends.

4. Using the TWO-STITCH TWISTED ROSE (page 16), make clusters of roses from rose shades of 4mm heirloom sylk ribbon. Also stitch FRENCH KNOTS (page 14), forming buds. From 4mm light-green heirloom sylk ribbon, stitch RIBBON STITCHES (page 15), forming leaves.

5. Photocopy pattern onto mat board. Cut out opening and place over stitching. Place in frame.

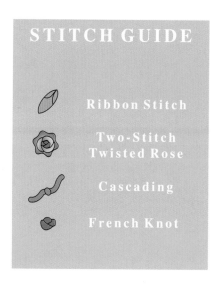

STITCH GUIDE

Ribbon Stitch

Two-Stitch
Twisted Rose

Cascading

French Knot

Spring Wreath Pattern

Summer Wreath Pattern

Autumn Wreath

Autumn Wreath

Stitches & Techniques
FRENCH KNOT
LAZY DAISY STITCH
RIBBON STITCH
STRAIGHT STITCH

Materials
Picture frame with a 6" x 7½" window
6½" x 8" piece of mat board
5" x 6" piece of striped cotton fabric
³/₈" decorative button
Two ½" brass leaf charms
4mm green heirloom sylk ribbon
4mm rust heirloom sylk ribbon
4mm tan heirloom sylk ribbon
3mm green rayon ribbon
3mm gold rayon ribbon
Disappearing-ink fabric marker
Large-eyed needle (darner)
Beading needle and floss
Scissors
Craft glue
Color photocopy machine

Directions

1. Using the transfer method of your choice (page 13), lightly transfer the design onto the fabric with the fabric marker.

2. Stitch STRAIGHT STITCHES (page 16) in a clockwise direction around with 3mm green and gold rayon ribbons, forming the wreath.

3. Stitch clusters of three RIBBON STITCHES (page 15) around wreath with 4mm green and tan heirloom sylk ribbon. Stitch FRENCH KNOTS (page 14) with 4mm rust heirloom sylk ribbon.

4. Glue leaf charms to the top of the wreath. Tie a small bow with a short length of rust ribbon. Glue bow to the center of the charms.

5. Stitch three LAZY DAISY STITCHES (page 15) with 4mm rust heirloom sylk ribbon, forming door hinges. Glue the button in place for the doorknob.

6. Photocopy pattern onto mat board. Cut out opening and place over stitching. Place in frame.

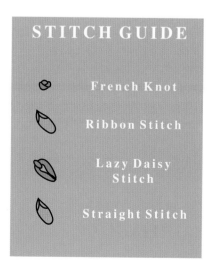

STITCH GUIDE

French Knot

Ribbon Stitch

Lazy Daisy Stitch

Straight Stitch

Winter Wreath

Winter Wreath

Stitches & Techniques
TWO-STITCH TWISTED ROSE

Materials
Picture frame with a 6" x 7$\frac{1}{2}$" window
6$\frac{1}{2}$" x 8" piece of mat board
5" x 6" piece of lightweight cotton fabric
5" x 6" piece of fusible webbing
$\frac{1}{2}$" metal button
Two $\frac{1}{2}$" bells
1$\frac{1}{4}$" gold cherub charm
48" of $\frac{3}{8}$" gold decorative ribbon
51" of $\frac{1}{4}$" green sheer ribbon
$\frac{1}{4}$" metallic-gold ribbon
4mm white silk ribbon
51" length of 1mm green cording
Disappearing-ink fabric marker
Large-eyed needle (darner)
Needle and quilting thread
Scissors
Craft glue
Color photocopy machine

Directions
1. Cut the 48" of $\frac{3}{8}$" gold decorative ribbon into 6" strips. Place the strips side by side onto fusible webbing. Fuse the ribbon strips onto cotton fabric piece following manufacturer's instructions, forming door area.

2. Cut the 51" of green sheer ribbon into three equal lengths. Cut the 51" of 1mm green cording into three equal lengths. Layer the cording and ribbon lengths and braid together. Bring the ends together, forming a 1$\frac{1}{2}$" circle, and secure with quilting thread. Trim excess ribbon.

3. Wrap the circle with $\frac{1}{4}$" metallic-gold ribbon, as shown in photo; stitch ends together to secure. Center and hand-stitch circle to door area.

4. Using the transfer method of your choice (page 13), lightly transfer the design onto the fabric with the fabric marker.

5. Glue the cherub charm just above the ribbon circle. Glue the button in place for the doorknob.

6. Cut three 15" lengths of 4mm white silk ribbon. Handling all lengths as one, tie ribbon into a 1$\frac{1}{2}$" bow. Glue the bow to the top of the ribbon circle; tie each of the ribbon ends together and glue on either side of the wreath. Tie a short length of 4mm white silk ribbon to each bell. Stitch the ribbon on the opposite end of the bells in place under the bow at the center top of the ribbon circle.

7. Make a TWO-STITCH TWISTED ROSE (page 16) from 4mm white silk ribbon. Glue the rose to the center of the bow.

8. Photocopy pattern onto mat board. Cut out opening and place over stitching. Place in frame.

STITCH GUIDE

Two-Stitch
Twisted Rose

123

Autumn Wreath Pattern

Winter Wreath Pattern

Metric Equivalence Chart

MM-Millimetres   CM-Centimetres
INCHES TO MILLIMETRES AND CENTIMETRES

INCHES	MM	CM	INCHES	CM	INCHES	CM
1/8	3	0.3	9	22.9	30	76.2
1/4	6	0.6	10	25.4	31	78.7
1/2	13	1.3	12	30.5	33	83.8
5/8	16	1.6	13	33.0	34	86.4
3/4	19	1.9	14	35.6	35	88.9
7/8	22	2.2	15	38.1	36	91.4
1	25	2.5	16	40.6	37	94.0
1 1/4	32	3.2	17	43.2	38	96.5
1 1/2	38	3.8	18	45.7	39	99.1
1 3/4	44	4.4	19	48.3	40	101.6
2	51	5.1	20	50.8	41	104.1
2 1/2	64	6.4	21	53.3	42	106.7
3	76	7.6	22	55.9	43	109.2
3 1/2	89	8.9	23	58.4	44	111.8
4	102	10.2	24	61.0	45	114.3
4 1/2	114	11.4	25	63.5	46	116.8
5	127	12.7	26	66.0	47	119.4
6	152	15.2	27	68.6	48	121.9
7	178	17.8	28	71.1	49	124.5
8	203	20.3	29	73.7	50	127.0

YARDS TO METRES

YARDS	METRES	YARDS	METRES	YARDS	METRES	YARDS	METRES	YARDS	METRES
1/8	0.11	2 1/8	1.94	4 1/8	3.77	6 1/8	5.60	8 1/8	7.43
1/4	0.23	2 1/4	2.06	4 1/4	3.89	6 1/4	5.72	8 1/4	7.54
3/8	0.34	2 3/8	2.17	4 3/8	4.00	6 3/8	5.83	8 3/8	7.66
1/2	0.46	2 1/2	2.29	4 1/2	4.11	6 1/2	5.94	8 1/2	7.77
5/8	0.57	2 5/8	2.40	4 5/8	4.23	6 5/8	6.06	8 5/8	7.89
3/4	0.69	2 3/4	2.51	4 3/4	4.34	6 3/4	6.17	8 3/4	8.00
7/8	0.80	2 7/8	2.63	4 7/8	4.46	6 7/8	6.29	8 7/8	8.12
1	0.91	3	2.74	5	4.57	7	6.40	9	8.23
1 1/8	1.03	3 1/8	2.86	5 1/8	4.69	7 1/8	6.52	9 1/8	8.34
1 1/4	1.14	3 1/4	2.97	5 1/4	4.80	7 1/4	6.63	9 1/4	8.46
1 3/8	1.26	3 3/8	3.09	5 3/8	4.91	7 3/8	6.74	9 3/8	8.57
1 1/2	1.37	3 1/2	3.20	5 1/2	5.03	7 1/2	6.86	9 1/2	8.69
1 5/8	1.49	3 5/8	3.31	5 5/8	5.14	7 5/8	6.97	9 5/8	8.80
1 3/4	1.60	3 3/4	3.43	5 3/4	5.26	7 3/4	7.09	9 3/4	8.92
1 7/8	1.71	3 7/8	3.54	5 7/8	5.37	7 7/8	7.20	9 7/8	9.03
2	1.83	4	3.66	6	5.49	8	7.32	10	9.14

Index